THE
WOOD
WORKER'S
MANUAL

THE
WOOD WORKER'S
MANUAL

GOSTA VASS

OVER 30 ILLUSTRATED STEP-BY-STEP PROJECTS

Grange
BOOKS

© 1987 Streiffert & Co./Johnston Editions

Published by Grange Books
An Imprint of Books & Toys Ltd
The Grange
Grange Yard
LONDON SE1 3AG

Reprinted 1992

ISBN: 1 85627 252 4

Filmset by Bokstaven, Gothenburg, Sweden
Lithography by Repro-Man, Gothenburg, Sweden
Printed and bound in Italy
by arrangement with Graphicom S.r.L., Vicenza

British Library Cataloguing in Publication Data
Vass, Gösta
    The woodworker's manual: over 30 fully
    illustrated step-by-step projects.
    1. Woodwork
    I. Title
    684'.08   TT180

Project editor and designer: Nils Hermanson
Translated by: Rosetta Translations, London
Copy editor: Jon C. van Leuven
Illustrators: Anders Engström, Hans Linder,
Lennart Molin, Ulf Söderqvist

CONTENTS

Wood and woodworking

TIMBER

To be quite sure about the quality of the timber you are going to work with, you can, if you have the opportunity, go the whole hog and fell and season your own timber. If, like most of us, you have to buy your timber at the lumber yard, the following is what happens with the timber before you get it.

Winter is the best time for felling all trees except birch, which should be felled at the height of its growth season, when it is in full leaf. (Birch is then left until the leaves have withered, so that the sap has gone and the wood is lighter in colour and drier.)

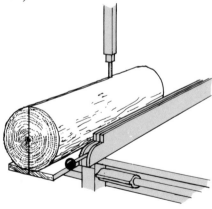

You yourself can saw up small tree stocks and lightish lumber in a band-saw, to your own requirements. If the tree stocks are heavy or many, then let a local sawmill do it for you.

When you saw the first cut in a round log, nail a plank to the bottom of the log, to stop it from rotating and to provide a surface for it to glide on. Avoid the nails when you saw the first cut! Then you simply need to make the second and following cuts at right angles to the first.

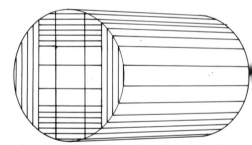

As a rule, the heavier planks (known as half timbers) are taken from the centre of the log, and the lighter planks—boards—are taken from the outer part.

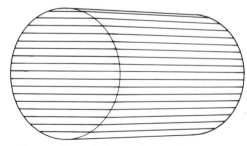

Through-and-through sawing consists of cutting the log in slices along its entire length and results in little waste.

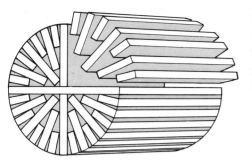

Quarter-sawn (the log is sawn in half and then in quarters) wood has more waste but, when seasoned, is much more stable than through-and-through sawn wood.

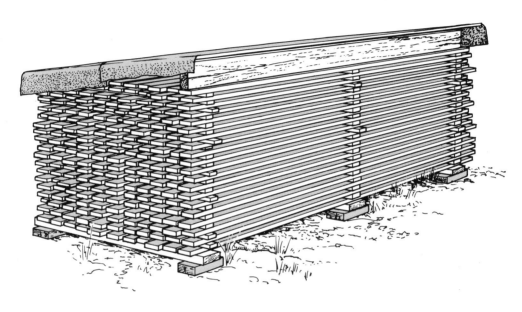

Buying and storing wood

Always buy your wood well in advance. This means that you need to forward-plan your woodworking projects, so that you know what kind of wood you need to buy. Wood that has not been kiln-dried or dried naturally has to dry properly, and this can take up to six months for dimensions up to 40 mm (1½″), and maybe up to a year for heavier dimensions. Generally, one can say that harder and more compact timber takes longer to season. It is important that wood is allowed to dry slowly, otherwise the ends tend to split badly, rendering the wood useless for woodworking.

Do not work with wood that you suspect is not dry enough—a short time in a centrally heated room and a piece of furniture made with insufficiently seasoned wood will have split and warped beyond repair.

For fresh timber, a cool, well-ventilated, covered-in space is the best first stop. Lay up the timber with stickers in between, to prevent warping. Suitable sticker dimensions are 20×40 mm (¾″×1½″) and the distance between the stickers should not exceed 1 metre (3′). Furthermore, the stickers should be straight above each other, otherwise the timber can become wavy, due to the uneven weighting. A final word about stickers— they should be of the same species of wood as that being dried. Otherwise, you can get stick stain, an ugly and sometimes deep colour mark in the wood. The one exception is birch which should be stickered with beech.

Protect the timber pile from variations of temperature, for example from strong sunlight. If the pile is outdoors, it must be covered against rain, too. The cover must be angled to the ground, so that condensation on the inside will flow off, instead of dropping on the upper planks.

To prevent heavier planks from splitting at the ends, you can give the ends a coating of glue or paint.

Even if the wood has been seasoned, it is a wise precaution to lay it up indoors for a couple of months, so that it acclimatizes to the ambient temperature and humidity.

Seasoned wood must also be laid up properly, on a flat floor with stickers of masonite or suchlike.

Buy your wood in the late autumn, during the winter, or in the early spring, to avoid fungi and sap stains. Certain species of wood are more sensitive than others to fungal decay and mould. Beech and birch are very sensitive and should be laid up in a very well-ventilated place with considerably thicker stickers than recommended above.

Remove bark from all timber that is being laid up for seasoning. Insects lay their eggs underneath the bark and the larvae can, when hatched, ruin your timber and even spread to other wood in the vicinity.

Metals and gases can cause discoloration to certain species of wood; for example, oak is discoloured by iron or ammonia. Don't store your oak in a henhouse or a stable, where there is quite a lot of ammoniac.

Choosing wood for your woodworking projects

Coniferous wood that is suitable for woodworking has very close annual growth rings, indicating that the wood is hard. (The tighter the rings, the tougher the wood.) The opposite is the case with deciduous timber—it is the fastest growing trees that have the hardest wood.

Certain types of ornamental bushes and fruit trees have excellent wood for the carpenter, for example, laburnum, lilac, cherry, apple, blackthorn, and pear. The colour of cherry wood varies from light yellow to violet, while laburnum, an extremely hard wood, has a yellow-white surface and a dark brown heartwood. Pear wood varies from pink to yellowish, and apple from yellow to brown. All fruit trees have smooth wood with no pores, and they are easy to turn and even to work with hand tools.

Finally, some tips to remember when you visit the lumber yard.

★ Coniferous wood should have close growth rings.

★ Deciduous wood should have sparse growth rings. Check especially to see if there are split ends!

★ Check that the planks are straight. Twisted planks have a built-in tension that cannot be removed.

★ Check that the wood does not have dead knots, which can easily become loose and drop out.

★ It is normal that planks have end splitting. Buy longer planks than you need, so that you can saw off the split parts.

★ Choose planks cut from the same log, if possible. Otherwise, choose planks with similar growth rings, that is, planks that are taken from about the same place in the log.

WOODWORKING TOOLS

A complete basic tool kit is vital if you are going to produce work of good quality. Nothing is more frustrating than trying to carry out some operation with tools that were not meant for it, so time and money spent in acquiring a good tool kit is never wasted. In the following section, we cover all these tools. In the projects that follow later on in this book, we do not list the "normal" tools (hammer, screwdriver, and suchlike) under the head-ing "Tools", but instead we mention the more or less specialized tools or machines that are needed for the project in question.

To produce the best results, all edged woodworking tools should be sharp. Dull tools are dangerous because they require too much force. Careless handling can also lead to injury and, if the tool is a power machine, might leave you handless . . . But nobody gets hurt if he or she is alert and careful, and if the tools are kept sharp and in good running order.

Therefore, the guards on circular saws, routers, and planers/jointers should always be used. Unfortunately, the guards on most circular saws are clumsy to work with, especially when cutting grooves or rebates, and many people remove them. If you do, *always* use a push stick to move the workpiece towards the blade, and be even more careful than usual.

Saws

Buy saws with unhardened teeth. You can then set and file the teeth to suit the kind of sawing that you will mainly be doing.

1. Handsaw with straight teeth, for cutting across and along the grain. Also known as a universal saw. 7 teeth per inch, 600 mm (4") long.
2. Tenon saw with universal teeth, 11 teeth per inch.
3. Dovetail saw with a bent and folding handle. 16 teeth per inch.
4. Coping saw, frame depth 150 mm (6").
5. Bowsaw with tensioning screws. With an 8 mm (¼") fretsaw blade and a 30 mm (1") blade for cutting dovetails.
6. Saw-file.
7. Saw-set. A tool for setting saw teeth.
8. Mitre box.

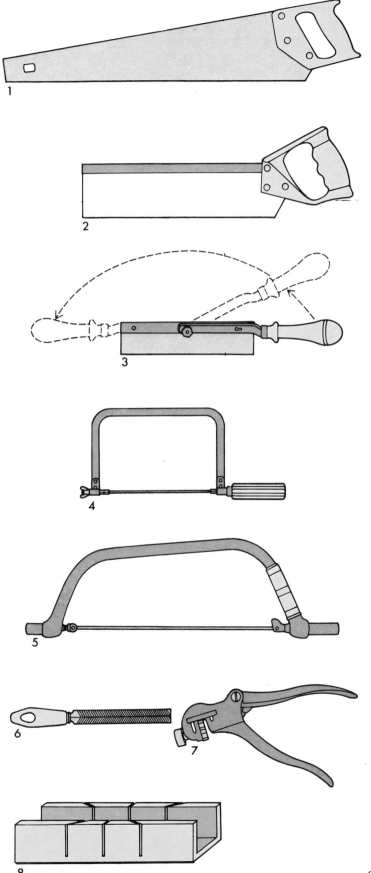

9

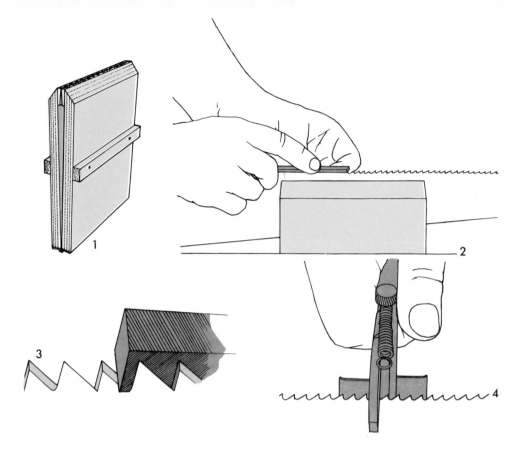

How to sharpen and set a saw

Only saws whose points have not been hardened can be sharpened and set. The sharpening tool is a triangular singlecut, fine saw-file of a size that suits the saw in question.

1. Cushion the saw between two strips of planed timber, so that its teeth protrude about 10–15 mm (½″).

2. Begin by topping, that is, filing all the teeth to the same height by running a flat file over them a few times. The teeth have now got flattened points.

3. Start now at the back of the saw (the handle end) and file the teeth that are set from the side you are standing on, that is, the teeth which are bent away from you. File all the teeth on their front faces and then on the rear faces. Hold the file at right angles to the blade and at the angle that the teeth had originally. It will help if you draw this angle across the tops of the wooden strips with a bevel gauge, and "follow" the line with your eye.

File the teeth until the flattened top of each tooth that bends away from you has become a point, and all the points have the same height.

Turn the saw around and repeat the procedure.

4. With all the teeth now filed, it is time to set the teeth, that is, bend them out of the perpendicular so that the cut is wider than the blade, thus giving the blade clearance as it is moved through the wood. This is done with a saw-set. Count the number of teeth per inch, and adjust the saw-set to this figure. Place the set over the first tooth and press firmly. Repeat for all teeth set away from the side you are standing on, turn the saw, and set all the other teeth.

When cutting wood that is damp, you can well use a saw that is set more than normal, but don't exaggerate the set, as this will leave a much rougher cut, which eats up more material and thus slows down the work.

Planes

Before you buy a plane, check how the blade, or cutting iron, is fitted. It should be adjustable both laterally and vertically, and the cap iron should fit snugly up to it, breaking the shaving smoothly and quickly.

1. Jack plane of iron, with smooth sole, 335–450 mm (14–18″) long and 50–60 mm (2–2½″) wide. If you are planing a wide piece of wood, use the longest model.

2. Spokeshave, with two screws for adjusting the cutter. This is indispensable when rounding irregular and curved shapes.

3. Smoothing plane, also of iron and with a smooth sole, 240 mm (10″) long and 50 mm (2″) wide. The smooth sole is preferable to the corrugated, as the latter type tends to steer along the corrugations when you are planing edges.

Chisels and gouges

1. You need a set of chisels of various widths, say, 6, 10, 12, 16, 20, and 25 mm (¼″, ⅜″, ½″, ⅝″, ¾″ and 1″). Choose wooden handles, as wood is more comfortable to hold. Plastic handles are tougher, of course.

2. Gouge. You will need two gouge sizes, 6 mm (¼″) and 25 mm (1″).

Knives

1. Sheath knife of hardened steel. The blade should not be too long, and there must be a finger guard.

2. Universal knife with replaceable blade.

3. Woodwork knife.

4. Veneer saw.

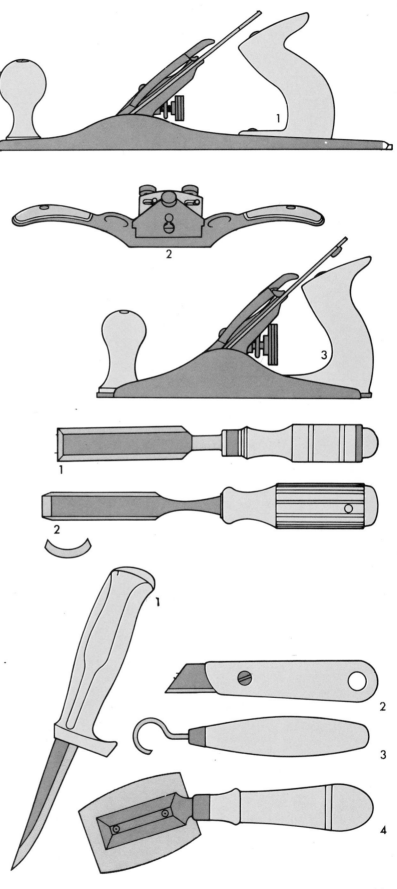

Grinding

Neglect and careless handling cause dull edges. Apart from the fact that dull tools will not produce the best results, they are, as we have said, potentially dangerous. The good workman takes care of his tools.

Many woodworkers use a powered emery wheel for sharpening their tools. This is used dry, and the heat generated can draw the temper from the steel, so it must be dipped regularly in water. If you have room for it in your workroom, a traditional power-driven grindstone (see page 21) on a stand is a sound investment. It will last a lifetime, if properly cared for. Its surface is permanently saturated with water, which keeps the stone clean, and the low speed of the machine means that it will not overheat the steel.

When you buy a grindstone, you should insist on trying it out first. Pick a grindstone with a diameter of at least 450 mm (18") and a thickness of 70 mm (2¾"). The surface should not be too rough—a medium grit size (180) is best.

It is not good for the grindstone to stand too long in water, so the trough should be lowerable or have a plug through which you can tap off the water.

When you use the grinding stone, it is a good idea to have an emery wheel to start with. Rough grind on the emery wheel, if the tool edge to be ground is jagged. Check that the bevel is square at the top. Then go over to the grindstone.

You must take good care of your grindstone. If its surface becomes jagged, use a grindstone dresser to produce a new, smooth surface. To clean the stone from previously ground particles, hold an ordinary brick against the surface while the stone is rotating.

Avoid grinding axes and suchlike on the grindstone. Use the emery wheel instead.

The emery wheel runs at a much higher speed than does the grindstone, and the resulting high temperatures can remove the temper of the steel, so it is important that you do not exert too much pressure between blade and wheel, and that you cool the blade often by dipping it in water. "Bluing" is the telltale sign of loss of temper.

Keeping the emery wheel clean is important, so you need to have a suitable dresser for regular cleaning.

1. When using the emery wheel, always rest the tool on the tool rest, which you adjust to the required angle. This helps you to put the correct pressure on the tool.

The beginner will always find it difficult to obtain a straight and even bevel, but he can practise with the broadest chisel or plane cutting-iron. Set the tool rest at an angle of 30 degrees. Move the bevel to and fro against the disc while maintaining light pressure. Dip the steel in water often. Continue grinding until you get a burr, or wire edge, along the entire length of the bevel. You are now ready to finish the job by honing the bevel on an oil stone.

2. The most suitable oil stone is a combination stone of carborundum— one surface is rough and one fine. Use a honing guide to produce the correct bevel angle. For the finest edge, finish with an Arkansas stone.

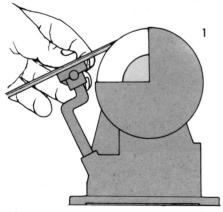

1

Always use safety goggles when grinding on an emery wheel.

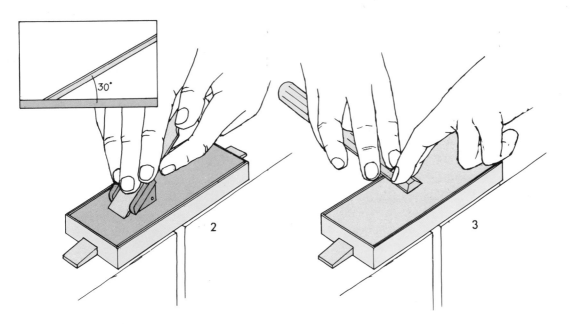

Keep the oil stone in a suitable plastic box, so that the edge of the stone is proud of the top edge of the box. Then you can use the stone without taking it out of its box. The stone should be kept in a light mineral oil—sewing-machine oil is fine—so there should be some space between the stone and the box.

Put the tool in the honing guide and start on the rough side. Hold the bevel so that its entire length is on the stone, press gently and move the bevel to and fro.

3. Then turn the blade flat on its back and rub gently until the burr is removed. Repeat the procedure on the fine side of the oil stone. When you hone planing irons, give the bevel a slight convex shape, so that the corners of the blade do not dig into the wood.

Cabinet scrapers

1. A simple rectangular blade of polished steel, which is an indispensable tool for making a finish on a hardwood surface. Choose a blade of the best quality, and it can be used for ever, being capable of being sharpened again and again. A rectangular scraper, say 125×60 mm (5×2¼″), is best. It should be, say, 1 mm thick (¹⁄₂₄″).

2. A swan- or goose-necked scraper of approximately the same dimensions is necessary for round shapes.

3. Scraper sharpener, for trimming and polishing the scraper's blade.

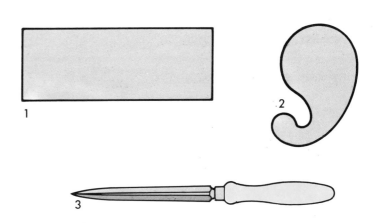

Sharpening a cabinet scraper

Hold the scraper in a vice, and sharpen one edge at a time. Begin by filing the edge with a fine saw-file until the hooked burr, which has become dull, has been filed square and flat. Do this by holding the file in both hands and drawing it at right angles firmly across the edge a few times. Remove any burr caused by this part of the operation with a few light strokes of the file.

To give the scraper its hooked burr, use a scraper-sharpener and a few drops of oil to lubricate it. Take the sharpener in both hands and firmly draw it over the blade at a slight angle, until you get a good burr on each side of the blade.

When the blade dulls again, you can recondition it simply without having to repeat the above procedure. Simply hold the scraper at an angle of about 30 degrees to a flat piece of hard wood and, with the point of the scraper-sharpener in one end of the little hook, draw the sharpener firmly along the edge of the burr. This will put a new edge on the cabinet scraper. Draw the sharpener at a slight angle along the hook, to give the scraper its fine edge again. You can recondition like this up to five or six times, before you need to file down the top and sharpen as above.

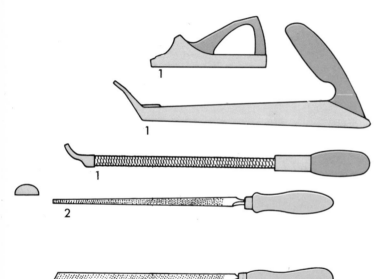

Smoothing tools

1. Surform rasp tools with replaceable blades. These can be used either with or against the grain.
2. Cabinet rasp. Half-round section, 300 mm (12″) long and 34 mm (1⅜″) wide. This is for very coarse work before a file is used; for instance, when doing the quick, preliminary rounding of a workpiece. It has pocket-shaped teeth.

Files

1. Standard file with flat blade, 100–350 mm (4–14″).
2. Cabinetmaker's half-round file, 300×28.5 mm (12×1⅛″).
3. Round file. Medium, 300 mm (12″) long and with a diameter of 12.5 mm (½″).

Drills

The widespread use of power drills has made the traditional woodworker's brace less common.
1. Hand drill. Many woodworkers use only power drills, but the hand drill, with a chuck capacity of up to 6 mm (¼ inch), is sometimes just as quick to use.

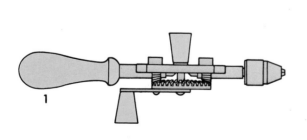

2. Set of solid-centre auger bits with combination shanks for both power drill and brace. Also known as the Jennings-pattern bit. The set should include 12, 16, 20 and 25 mm (½″, ⅝″, ¾″, and 1″) bits.

3. Twist drills, a set from 1–10 mm (1/32–⅜″).

4. You are also going to need a drill with an expanding bit, to bore holes of varying diameters.

5. Bradawl.

6. Piercing awl.

7. Countersinker.

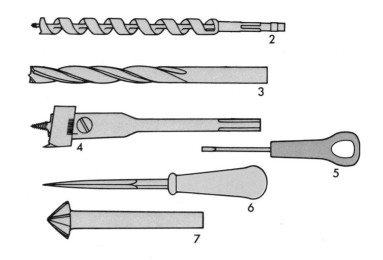

Screwdrivers

The important thing about a screwdriver is that the blade fits the screw slot correctly. Too big or too little a blade, and the slot may be damaged. And worse, it is very easy for it to slip out and damage the surface of the timber. The shape of the handle is a matter of personal preference, the important thing being that you can get a firm grip on it.

1. Screwdriver bits with the straight, traditional blade, 4, 6, and 8 mm (5/32″, ¼″, and 5/16″).

2. Philips screwdriver head.

3. Pozidrive screwdriver head.

4. A screwdriver bit holder is more versatile than the ordinary screwdriver.

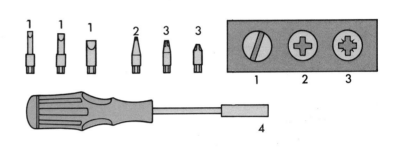

Hammers

1. Carpenter's hammer, preferably with steel handle, (675 g/16 oz). This type, also called the clawhammer, is indispensable for carpentry.

2. Cross pein hammer, (150 g/4 oz). The wedge-shaped pein is used for starting brads or light nails in cabinet work.

3. Round wooden mallet. This shape is preferable to the more traditional, flat-faced mallet, as it actually makes it easier to get a clean strike on the chisel handle.

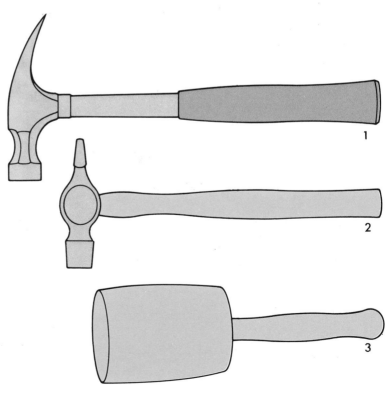

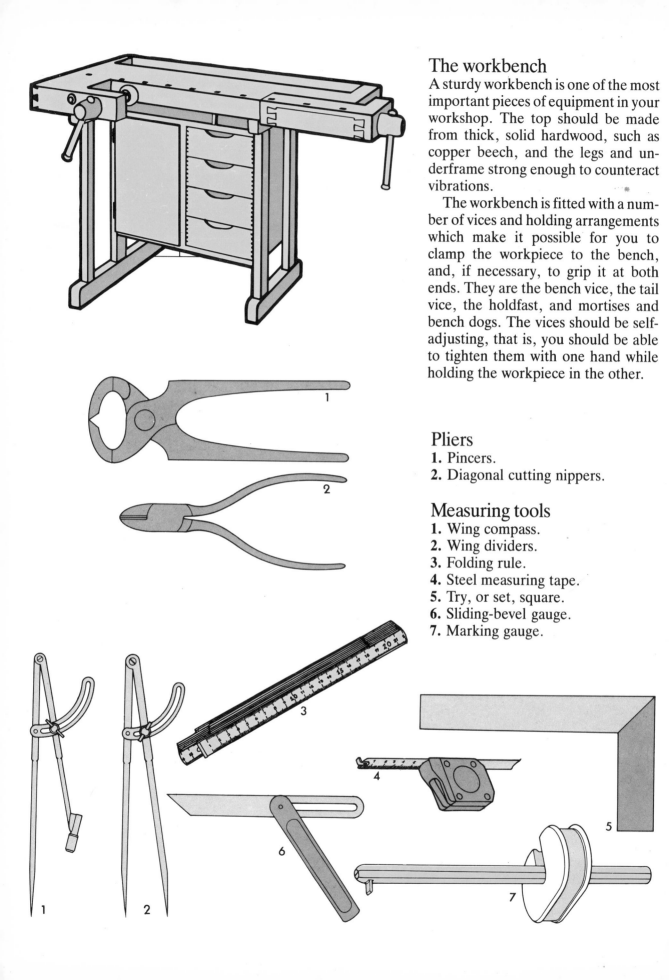

The workbench

A sturdy workbench is one of the most important pieces of equipment in your workshop. The top should be made from thick, solid hardwood, such as copper beech, and the legs and underframe strong enough to counteract vibrations.

The workbench is fitted with a number of vices and holding arrangements which make it possible for you to clamp the workpiece to the bench, and, if necessary, to grip it at both ends. They are the bench vice, the tail vice, the holdfast, and mortises and bench dogs. The vices should be self-adjusting, that is, you should be able to tighten them with one hand while holding the workpiece in the other.

Pliers
1. Pincers.
2. Diagonal cutting nippers.

Measuring tools
1. Wing compass.
2. Wing dividers.
3. Folding rule.
4. Steel measuring tape.
5. Try, or set, square.
6. Sliding-bevel gauge.
7. Marking gauge.

Holding tools

A woodworker can never have too many cramps, so buy several in each size. There are many other types of cramps than those shown here, such as G-cramps, edge cramps, and T-bar cramps, but the selection suggested here is sufficient for all the projects in the book.

1. Adjustable cramps are excellent for one-handed operation and can accommodate many thicknesses of wood. You should have at least three sizes: 150 mm (6″), 200 mm (7″), and 250 mm (9″).

2. Cramp bands, for holding box or frame constructions together while they are being glued. Also known as a web cramp. This replaces the older cord/rope tourniquet. It is usually used in conjunction with blocks of wood that are pressed out towards the corners of the frame, to increase the pressure.

3. Sash cramps. These are expensive, but vital for the assembly of cabinet-work.

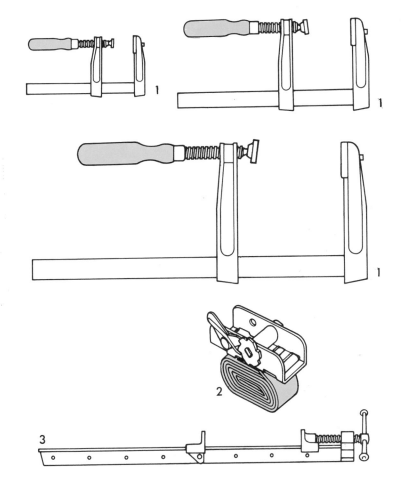

Grinding equipment

1. Combination oil stone with one side in medium grit and the other in fine grit.

2. Arkansas stone. Apart from being expensive, it is difficult to get hold of, but well worth the price and effort, as it produces the very best finish.

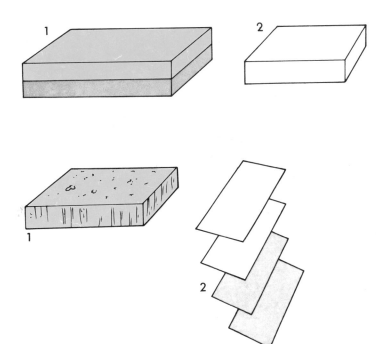

Sanding equipment

Although we talk about sanding and sand paper still, smoothing and abrasive paper are the more correct terms.

1. Sanding block. This helps you to produce an even surface.

2. Abrasive paper, aluminium oxide.

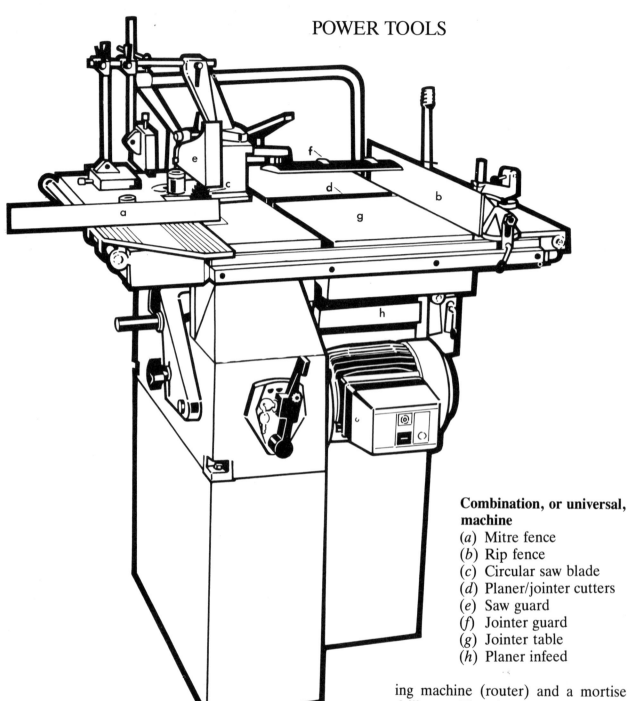

Combination, or universal, machine
- (*a*) Mitre fence
- (*b*) Rip fence
- (*c*) Circular saw blade
- (*d*) Planer/jointer cutters
- (*e*) Saw guard
- (*f*) Jointer guard
- (*g*) Jointer table
- (*h*) Planer infeed

Combination, or universal, machine

This is invaluable, as it gives the woodworker a range of functions while taking up relatively little space in the workroom. Three functions are a must: circular saw, planer and jointer, while you very often get a vertical milling machine (router) and a mortise drill, too. The planer and jointer are exceptionally useful, as you can save a lot of money by producing your own finished planks, instead of having to buy them ready-finished from the lumber yard. You should be able to change from one function to another and go back again without having to re-do the settings you had on the first function. You may, of course, buy each machine separately.

The circular saw

When sawing thin pieces on the circular saw, adjust the height of the blade so that it is only 5 mm (³⁄₁₆″) higher than the workpiece. Have a number of push sticks available, 200 mm (8″) long and about 15 mm (½″) thick at the handle end, narrowing down to about 8 mm (¼″) at the blade end (see drawing). Birch and beech are suitable materials. Drill a hole in the handles and have the push sticks hanging within reach of the machine.

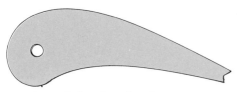

Push stick for the circular saw.

When ripping a plank, you use the rip fence as guide, holding the long edge of the plank against it while you move the short edge towards the saw blade. NEVER pull the plank towards you, once you have started feeding it past the blade. Instead, you must push the plank past the blade, lift it up, and bring it back to the starting position.

When crosscutting on the circular saw, the workpiece is held or clamped against the mitre fence, at right angles to the blade, and both are moved towards the blade. A stop block is a must when you are crosscutting. This allows the pieces to move freely on the diagonal between the blade and the rip fence.

NEVER use the circular saw without a fence. If you have to work without a fence, then use the bandsaw instead.

The jointer/planer

This is a combined machine, in which the jointer first gives one face of a rough board a smooth, flat surface. The workpiece is then put through the planer, which gives the board an all-over even thickness.

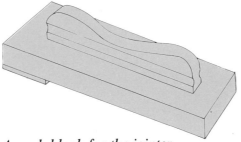

A push block for the jointer.

When using a jointer, the guard must always cover the complete width of the cutters, with just enough space between the guard and the workpiece to allow it to pass. A push-block should always be used to run the workpiece over the jointer's cutters. This usually has an extra block fixed to the end as a lip, to engage the end of the workpiece and push it along.

When one face is flat and smooth, one or both of the edges are usually jointed. The cutter guard must be lowered all the way down over the cutters and moved to the side only the thickness of the workpiece. In this way, the edge of the workpiece can be passed over the only section of the cutters that is bare.

NEVER joint pieces shorter than 250 mm (10″).

Keep the blades clean from wood resin with acetone or thinner. Workpieces will slide easily if you oil the jointer table lightly.

The planer feeds the plank through the machine automatically. You simply push it in at one end and out comes a plank at the other end, with an even thickness, as the planer uses the flat surface you produced on the jointer and then planes the opposite face parallel.

For the sake of simplicity, we use the terms "to plane" and "planer" as synonyms for "to joint" and "jointer" in the projects described in this book. Some people may not have a jointer/planer but will use a hand plane to produce the required flat surface.

19

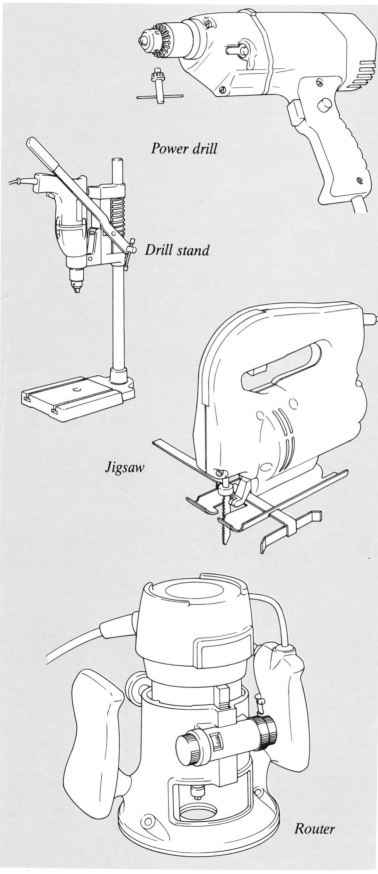

Power drill

Power drill

Drill stand

Jigsaw

Router

Power drill

You can have either a pillar drill or a portable power drill and drill stand. When drilling holes in wood with a pillar drill, or with a portable power drill in a drill stand, always clamp a workpiece thicker than about 10 mm (½"). Thinner pieces can be handheld, but many woodworkers prefer to clamp them anyway, as greater accuracy is easier to achieve with a clamped piece.

When drilling deep holes, remember to lift the drill out of the hole at intervals, so that the shavings don't fasten and the drill won't overheat. Remember also that the best results are obtained when you have a suitably high rotation speed and you move the drill through the workpiece with the correct speed.

Solid-centre auger bits produce the neatest and cleanest holes, and have the added advantage that they are less sensitive if you are drilling in material of varying hardness.

Jigsaw

Buy one with a roller support for the jigsaw blade and a sole plate that is adjustable in both planes, so that mitres up to 45° can be cut.

Router

Always use cutters of the best quality, and check that they are properly tightened before you start the machine. As the cutters rotate clockwise, the router will twist in that direction, so you should move the machine into the workpiece against the direction of rotation of the cutters.

The spindle rotates extremely fast, so great care is necessary. Don't cut too deeply with the router, as too much resistance slows down the motor.

A router capable of 24,000–30,000 rpm will be sufficient.

Orbital sander

A machine that produces about 25,000 rpm is sufficient for most smoothing jobs.

Bench grinder

The bench grinder consists of two emery wheels of different grits, one rough and one medium. See page 12 for instructions on how to use the emery wheel.

Bandsaw

The bandsaw is the least dangerous of all the tools, but you must always have the workpiece pressed to the bandsaw table. An adjustable guard covers the part of the blade that is not needed when cutting a piece of board of a certain width. The bandsaw is used to cut curves and irregular shapes, although it can be used for crosscutting.

Round workpieces must always be clamped or nailed to a plank so that they have something flat to rest on when they are fed past the blade and so that they don't start rotating under the force of the blade.

Grindstone

A worthwhile long-term investment for the amateur woodworker. See page 12 for advice on buying and maintaining a grindstone.

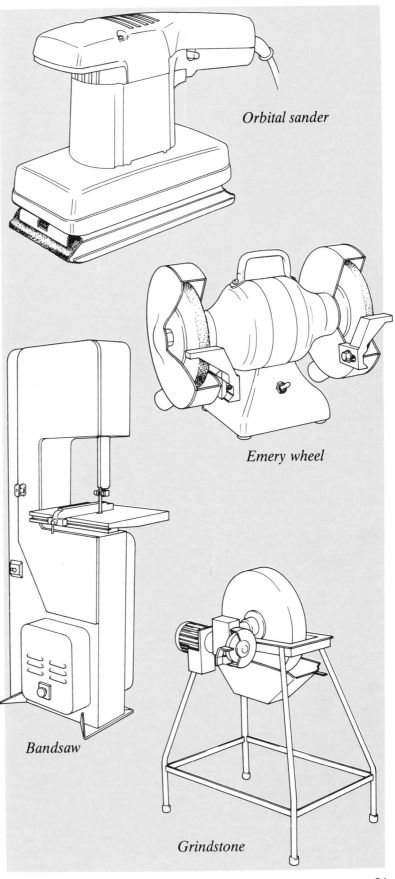

Orbital sander

Emery wheel

Bandsaw

Grindstone

Finishing

When the project you have been working on is ready, treating the surface will protect it and keep it fresh-looking.

Always brush the piece clean from sanding dust, etc. Never use a rag or paper.

Varnishing

Prime the surface with varnish diluted with 20–30% solvent. Read the instructions on the tin to find out what the solvent is.

Smooth down the surface when the varnish has dried. You can also use a cabinet scraper for this. Smoothing down will get rid of any particles in the varnish and also any wood fibres that have been raised by the varnish. Brush again.

Apply two coats of undiluted varnish, sanding down in between coats. Use long sweeping strokes when applying the varnish and work out over the edges.

You can give the final coat of varnish a mat surface by using fine steel wool and a mat polish.

Painting

Prime the brushed surface with primer or with paint diluted with solvent. Fill in cracks and uneven spots with painter's putty and sand it smooth. Brush again. Now apply a final coat of undiluted paint.

Oiling

An oiled surface looks natural and is water-repellent. Paraffin oil does not go rancid and is suitable for kitchen ware. Otherwise, boiled oil with 30% turpentine is suitable.

Apply the oil with a brush until the surface is drenched. Allow to stand for a while and then wipe off excess oil with a rag. Remember that turpentine and linseed oil can combust spontaneously, so drench them with water.

Glazing

Glaze should be oil-based. Proceed as for oiling. It is better to use a sponge rather than a brush.

Buy good-quality brushes for best results. But even good brushes shed their bristles in the beginning. Properly treated, a good brush will get better and better. Flat brushes are used most, but round ones are useful for painting into corners where plenty of paint is needed.

Painting pads spread an even coat on a smooth surface, but they have to be cleaned very well.

Clean your brushes immediately after use.

Clean them first in the paint solvent and, when they are really clean, wash them in soap and water.

Store your brushes upside down in a tin or jar, and cover them with a plastic bag to protect them from dust.

PROJECT PLANNING

Making a construction drawing

When you plan a project, a methodical approach is the best start. A scaled drawing will enable you to get a proper grip of the basic idea and of the intended proportions and dimensions. Going through the details at the planning stage will prepare you for the various problems that you are going to have to solve, and will also give you an exact idea of the materials you need. The scaled drawing will enable you to make a cutting list which you will need when buying the wood from the lumber yard. In the projects that follow, we have given nominal sizes, that is, the wood is not delivered finished (planed all round), but you must yourself cut and plane it to the exact dimensions. Wood in nominal sizes is cheaper than finished wood, and preparing the finished wood yourself enables you to produce exact dimensions at the same time as it gives you a better "feel" for the material.

Making a construction drawing of the project allows you to adapt the piece to suit your requirements. For instance, you might want to place this chest of drawers beside a table, and it would be aesthetically pleasing if they both had the same height. You must, therefore, add something to the height of the chest of drawers—or perhaps you will want to add a fourth drawer?

The chest of drawers (pages 96–103) Choose the biggest scale possible. A full-size drawing is best. This means that you can check the pieces by laying them on the drawing. However, full size is impractical. A scale of 1:2 fits the bill best, but if you want to work on a smaller scale you should not go below 1:5 (metric) or 1:4 (imperial).

The drawing must be accurate, so have good drawing tools—straight edges, set squares, an adjustable square, and a selection of lead pencils are usually enough to produce the necessary accuracy. Drawing on printed graph paper saves time.

Use broken lines to indicate joints and other hidden-from-view details that you want to note.

1

Make a plan drawing (a bird's eye view) of the top of the chest of drawers. Mark the length and the breadth of the top. Mark each of the individual strips that will be glued together to form the top. Mark out the cross members. Finally mark out with a broken line the tenons and grooves that will join the top and the cross members.

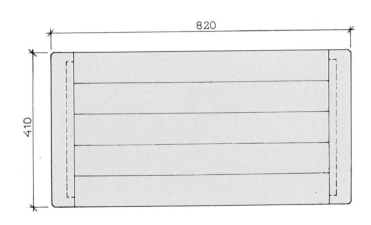

820

410

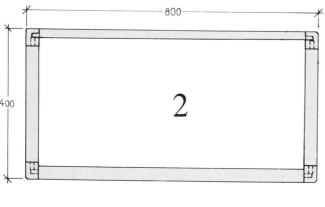

2

Draw a plan view of the carcase. Again, use broken lines to show the joints.

3

Draw a front view of the carcase, marking the positions of the drawer runners (*a*), the lower front rail (*b*), the upper front rail (*c*), and the upper and lower back rails (*d*).

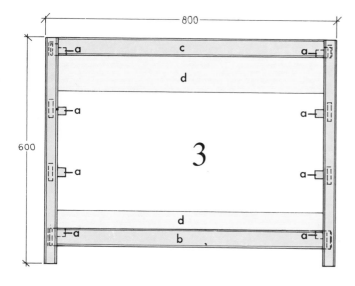

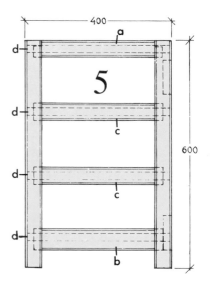

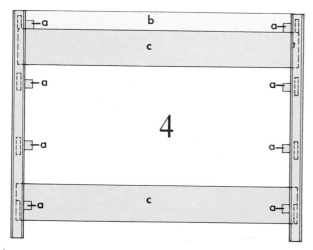

4

Draw a rear view of the carcase, marking in the runners (*a*), the upper front rail (*b*), the upper and lower back rails (*c*).

5

Draw a side view of the carcase, showing the upper (*a*) and lower (*b*) side rails and the two drawer guides (*c*), with broken lines showing the drawer runners (*d*) as well as the joints.

6

This cutaway front view is shown also on page 98, as it demonstrates how the exact position of the drawer guides (*a*) have to be measured. It also shows the drawer runners (*b*), the lippings (*c*) on the drawer bottoms (*d*), a rear post (*e*), the lower front rail (*f*), the upper front rail (*g*), and the drawer backs (*h*). The distances are marked in millimetres.

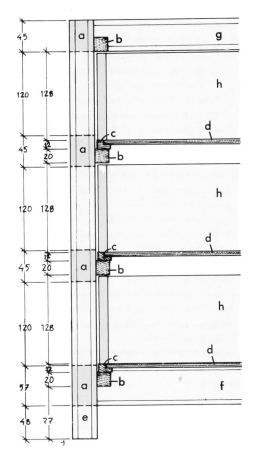

7

Draw the top view of the drawer.

8

Draw the front view of the drawer.

9

Draw the side view of the drawer.

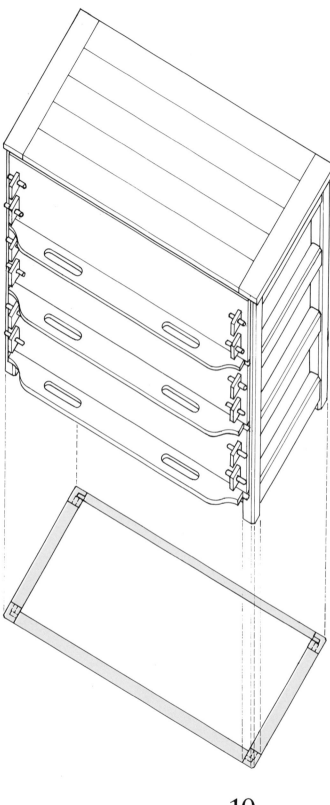

vertically and all horizontal lines at 30° to the horizontal.

Make a copy of the plan view of the chest top (step 2) on tracing paper and place it on the graph paper so that the front edge makes an angle of 30° to one of the horizontal lines on the graph paper. Draw vertical lines upwards from all crossing points on the top.

Mark off the vertical distances you require and then draw the other lines parallel to the projected top.

You now have an isometric projection, which will always appear distorted to the eye (isometric projections don't obey the laws of perspective). It does, however, allow you to consider the proportions of the various timber dimensions and to get a feel for the project as a whole.

11

Make full-size drawings of the more difficult details, especially the joints.

A
How the tenon on the drawer's back (*a*) slots into a groove in its side (*b*).

B
The drawer side (*a*) is joined to the drawer front (*b*) by a through mortise-and-tenon joint and locked with a dowel (*c*).

C
The drawer handle/front lipping (*a*) is grooved to take a tenon cut in the drawer bottom (*b*). The drawer front (*c*) is locked to the drawer side (*d*) by the tapered dowel (*e*).

D
Tenons are cut in the chest top (*a*) to fit in grooves routed in the cross member (*b*). This joint is not glued. Instead, a hole is drilled through the cross member and the tenon cheek and into the post (*c*) and the joint is locked with a dowel (*d*). The upper drawer runner (*e*) is shown attached to the post.

10

Now make a simple isometric projection. This is not so difficult. This projection shows all vertical lines

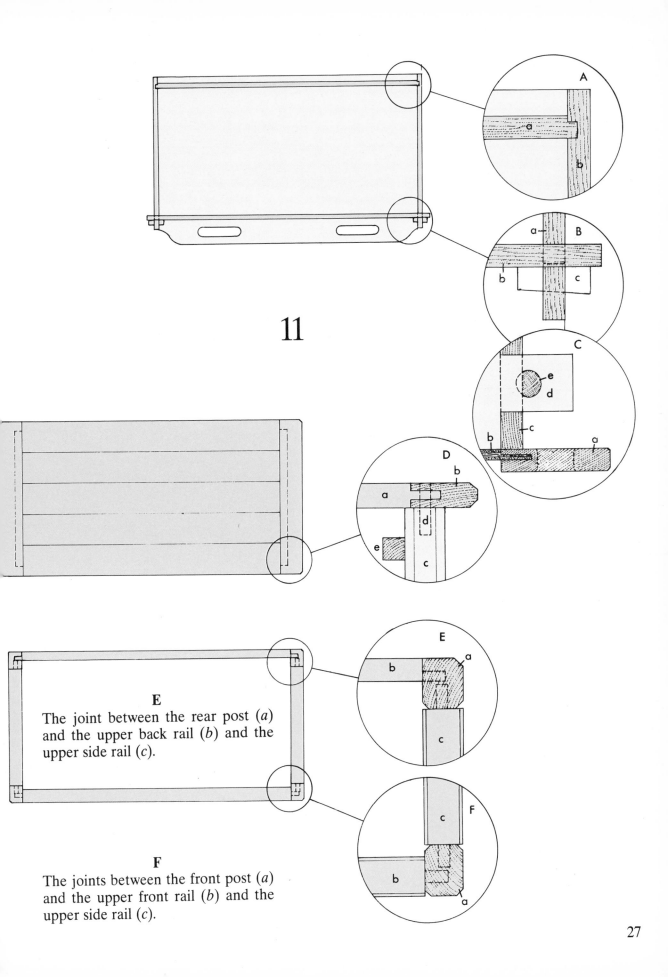

11

E
The joint between the rear post (*a*) and the upper back rail (*b*) and the upper side rail (*c*).

F
The joints between the front post (*a*) and the upper front rail (*b*) and the upper side rail (*c*).

27

BREADBOARD

MATERIAL
hardwood or softwood

TOOLS
standard combination handsaw
coping saw
smoothing plane
marking gauge
power drill with
    expanding bit, 25 mm (1″)

1

1

Cut the workpiece supporting the free end to prevent splitting.

Secure a suitably sized workpiece to the work table. Saw off the end, as the wood has often cracked or split there. Using the set square, draw a line at right angles to the long side, and continue it down over the edges.

Saw along the line, holding the saw almost horizontal and supporting the blade with the thumb of the other hand so that the first cut is straight. Then raise the saw to an almost vertical position, thus making the sawing more efficient.

Measure the desired length and cut the piece. When the cut is almost through, support the free end with your hand (see picture), or the wood will snap off and splinter.

2

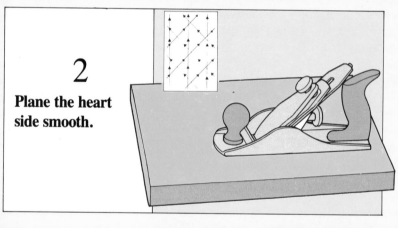

2

Plane the heart side smooth.

Secure the board on the bench with the heart side up, that is, the side which grew closest to the middle of the tree. Set the blade of the try plane fairly coarsely (about 1 mm or ⅟₃₂″). Plane diagonally, first in one direction and then in the other (see the arrows on the planing chart). When the board is flat, finish off with a few straight strokes with the blade set very fine.

3

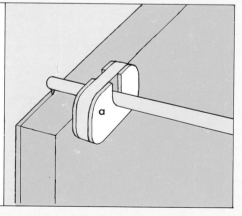

3

Mark the thickness of the breadboard and plane the other side.

Unfasten the workpiece and mark the desired thickness along the edge, using a marking gauge (*a*). Secure the board again, but with the unplaned side up. Plane the surface down to the mark, as described above.

4

Mark the rounded corners with the aid of a coin or suchlike. Cut with a coping saw, holding it vertically to ensure a vertical cut.

5

Use the power drill with expanding bit to make a hole for hanging. When the point of the bit just breaks through on the underside, turn the board over and drill through that side. This will produce a splinter-free hole.

6

Secure the workpiece to the bench again and smooth the long sides with the plane. The short sides can also be smoothed, but the blade must be set very finely indeed, since you are working across the grain. Plane from the end towards the middle.

7

Smooth the flat surfaces and edges with coarse abrasive paper until all plane marks have disappeared. Repeat with fine abrasive paper. Always smooth along the grain.

Finishing

Apply liquid paraffin with a clean cloth. When the wood has absorbed the oil it may swell, so smooth down with fine abrasive paper and finish off with another application of paraffin.

If the board becomes badly scarred after being in use for a time, smooth it down as described in point 6, and treat the surface again.

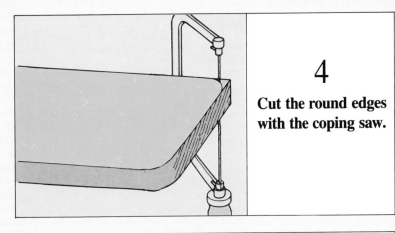

4

Cut the round edges with the coping saw.

5

Drill the hole from which the board will hang.

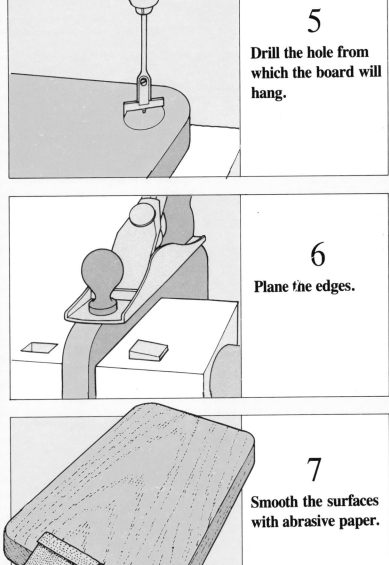

6

Plane the edges.

7

Smooth the surfaces with abrasive paper.

BOOT-JACK

MATERIAL
hardwood or plywood
leather

TOOLS
handsaw
bowsaw or fretsaw
plane
power drill
half-round file

Preparation

Trace the shape of the boot-jack on the wood, with the notch for the heel a little wider than a normal man's heel. The "tongue" of the jack must be long enough for you to stand on it with your other foot while pulling off a boot. The support underneath should raise the jack to allow a high-heeled boot to fit.

1

Cut the workpiece to length and shape.

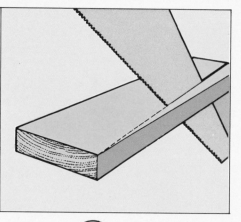

Cut the piece of wood to the right length. Secure it to a bench and saw out the conical shape, starting at the tongue end. Start with the saw at a small angle to the wood, so that the saw does not wander. When you get into the wood a little, raise the saw to cut more effectively.

2

Cut the heel notch with the bowsaw.

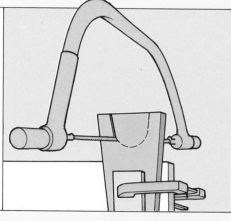

Secure the workpiece vertically. Cut the heel notch, using the bow- or fretsaw. The saw must move horizontally (perpendicular to the workpiece) so that both sides of the notch will have the same radius.

3

Saw the support. Secure it and bore the screw holes. Use a 4.5 mm (³⁄₁₆") drill to bore through, then countersink with a 10 mm (⅜″) drill until 20 mm (¾″) is left. Screw the support in place about 25 mm (1″) behind the notch. Cover the screws with paraffin wax before you screw them in.

4

Place the jack on a flat surface, and mark the angle of the toe and the support, using a straight piece of wood as a ruler. Secure the jack and plane off excess wood as far as the marked lines. The jack should now lie firmly on the floor.

5

Smooth down the notch with the file. Sand it to a smooth finish, always working the abrasive paper parallel to the grain of the wood.

6

Cut out a piece of leather somewhat wider than the jack. Draw a thin pencil line around the notch, as an outer limit for the glue. The leather should extend a little beyond this line on both sides of the jack. Spread glue on the wood and leather. Let it dry for the recommended time. Then fasten the leather against the inside rim of the notch, beginning at one end, pressing the leather firmly against the wood.

Now clip the leather to about 20 mm (¾″) from the rim at several points along the rim, so that it will open up to flatten smoothly. Press the leather against the top and bottom of the rim, starting from the middle. Shape the leather by pressing with the thumbs. Cut away excess leather with a sharp knife about 10 mm (⅜″) in from the rim.

Finishing
Treat the wood with paraffin wax or teak oil.

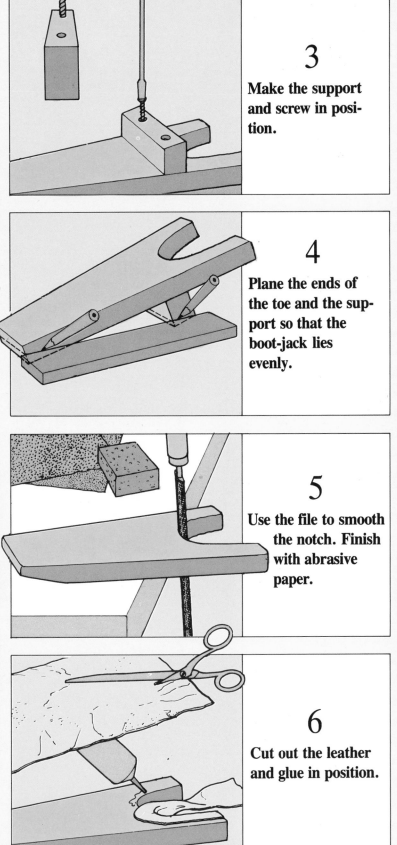

3
Make the support and screw in position.

4
Plane the ends of the toe and the support so that the boot-jack lies evenly.

5
Use the file to smooth the notch. Finish with abrasive paper.

6
Cut out the leather and glue in position.

JIGSAW PUZZLE

MATERIAL
birch plywood

TOOLS
handsaw
fretsaw

1

Cut two "layers" of plywood.

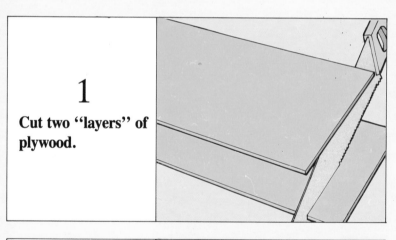

1

Using the handsaw, cut two sheets of plywood equal in size, according to the desired dimensions of the puzzle.

2

Draw the motif on one sheet, or stick on a picture.

2

Draw the selected motif on one of the sheets. Bear in mind that the transitions between the figures should be as unobtrusive as possible, so choose the shortest distance between the figures wherever practicable.

3

If you cannot draw the figures your-self, use a photo or a picture from a magazine, and stick the picture down with contact adhesive. The picture or drawing should be covered with a transparent varnish or fixative, avail-able in the paint shop.

3

Cover the motif with transparent varnish or fixative.

4

Use a cramp to secure the board on to a suitable surface, such as a table, and cut out the figures with the fretsaw. Be careful to hold the saw at right angles to the board to obtain a straight (verti-cal) cut. Note that the teeth should face downwards.

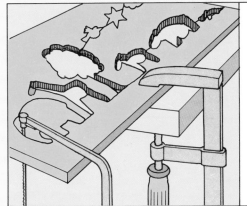

4

Cut out the pieces with a fretsaw.

5

Use the prepared sheet of plywood to trace the figures onto the other sheet. Apply contact adhesive to both the cut-out sheet and the whole one (but not where the figures have been marked). Allow to dry. Press the two pieces together, being especially care-ful when aligning the two surfaces—adjustments cannot be made later.

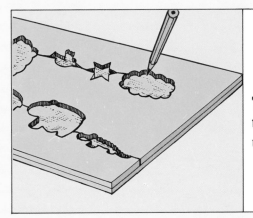

5

Trace the outline of the figures onto the uncut plywood.

6

Smooth down the sides, first with coarse abrasive paper and then with fine. Round off the sharp edges with abrasive paper.

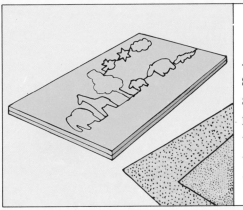

6

Apply contact adhe-sive to both sheets, avoiding the shapes marked on the whole sheet. Allow to dry and press together.

SAW-HORSE

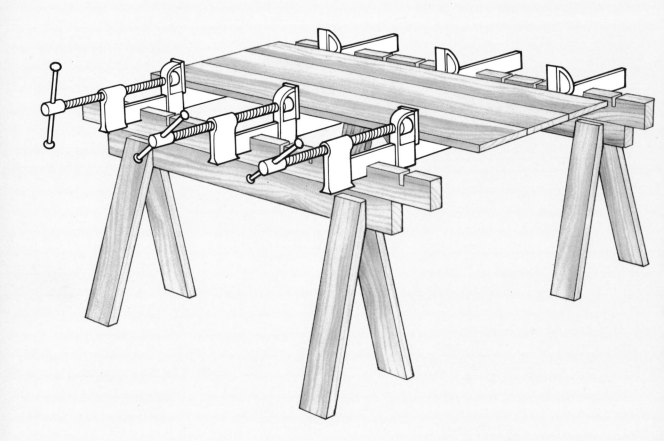

MATERIAL
pine

TOOLS
try plane
smoothing plane
handsaw
drill
marking gauge

Preparation
Start by cutting pieces for four legs
about 900 mm (3′) long and for a
crossbar 1,050 mm (3′ 6″) long, from a
plank of 50×100 mm (2″×4″) timber.

1

Secure one leg at a time in the workbench and plane one face and one edge. Check with a set square that the angle between face and edge is 90°. Repeat for the crossbar.

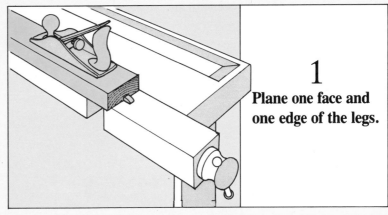

1

Plane one face and one edge of the legs.

2

Release the leg and mark a thickness of 45 mm (1¾") and a width of 95 mm (3¾") with the help of a marking gauge. Plane down to the marks. Repeat for the other legs and crossbar.

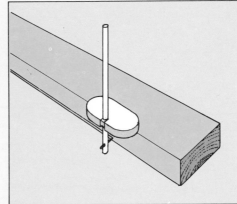

2

Mark up the thickness of the legs and plane to the mark.

3

Cut a squared-off end on each leg, using the handsaw. Start by marking a line at right angles across one face at the leg end, and continue the line around both edges.

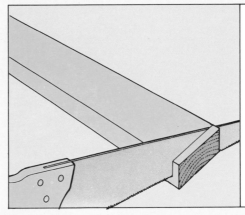

3

Square off the ends of the legs.

4

Mark the lap joint on each leg with a line at right angles (*a*), 90 mm (3¾") from the end. Measure 5 mm (3/16") from this line onto the thinner side of the leg, and draw a line (*b*) from there to a point 7 mm (¼") before the opposite edge on the leg's end. Thus (*b*) should slope at about 17°. Then continue (*b*) and, at right angles to it, mark a line (*c*) to join the original line (*a*) at the leg's corner.

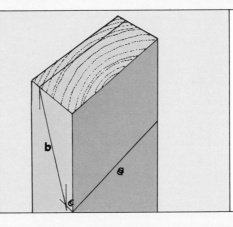

4

Mark the lap joint on each leg.

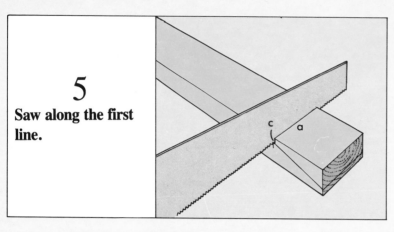

5

Saw along the first line.

5

Cut first along lines (a) and (c) at the same time.

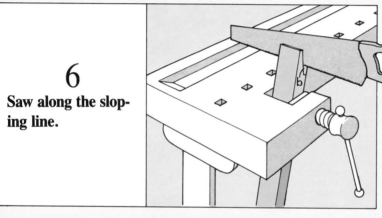

6

Saw along the sloping line.

6

Secure the leg in the work bench in such a way that the sloping line (b) becomes vertical, and saw along it. Repeat with the other legs.

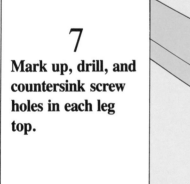

7

Mark up, drill, and countersink screw holes in each leg top.

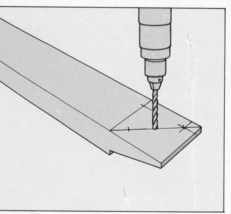

7

Mark three screw holes in a diagonal line (see picture). Drill with a 5 mm (³⁄₁₆″) bit and countersink. Note that the outer holes should be 25 mm (1″) from the corners. Round off all edges and corners, and smooth down the surfaces with abrasive paper.

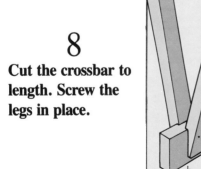

8

Cut the crossbar to length. Screw the legs in place.

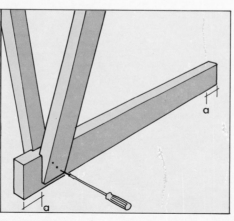

8

Mark and cut the crossbar to a length of 1 metre (39″). Make a thin pencil mark (a) 100 mm (4″) from the ends of the crossbar for the position of the legs. Secure the crossbar to the bench with a couple of cramps, then screw and glue on the legs. Be careful to fix the legs at right angles, and ensure they are bedded right down to the contact surface.

9

After having screwed on the legs, stand the saw-horse on the floor and use a 10 mm (³⁄₈″) wooden block to mark the bottoms of the legs so that they stand flat. Cut the legs along the marked lines with the handsaw, and check that the saw-horse is steady. Bevel all the legs with coarse abrasive paper to prevent them from splintering when pulled along the floor.

9

Mark up the floor angles and saw off the leg bottoms.

10

A detachable crossbar with notches for cramps can be made as an optional extra. It is useful when, for example, gluing together several boards without assistance.

The crossbar should be approximately 70 mm×45 mm×1200 mm (2³⁄₄″×1³⁄₄″×4′) with notches 6 mm×40 mm (¼″×1½″).

To position the notches, measure 50 mm (2″) in from both ends and then mark at 100 mm (4″) intervals. Make the notches with the handsaw. For this purpose a saw box is useful, i.e. a box with a slot at right angles in which the saw is guided.

10

Make a detachable crossbar. Saw out notches for cramps.

11

Place the detachable crossbar on the saw-horse so that the ends protrude 100 mm (4″) on each side. Secure with cramps, and drill with a 10 mm (³⁄₈″) bit right through the detachable crossbar and about 30 mm (1¼″) into the crossbar of the saw-horse. Then make dowels and glue them into the detachable crossbar with about 25 mm (1″) sticking out. Round off the ends of the dowels, to make it easier to fit the detachable crossbar into position on the saw-horse.

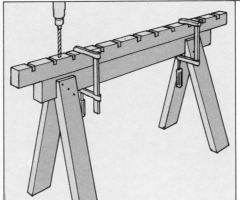

11

Drill holes through the detachable and saw-horse crossbars.

12

Finish off by smoothing down and bevelling all edges and corners — also the edges of the notches on the upper side of the detachable crossbar.

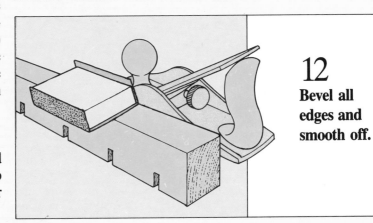

12

Bevel all edges and smooth off.

HOBBY-HORSE

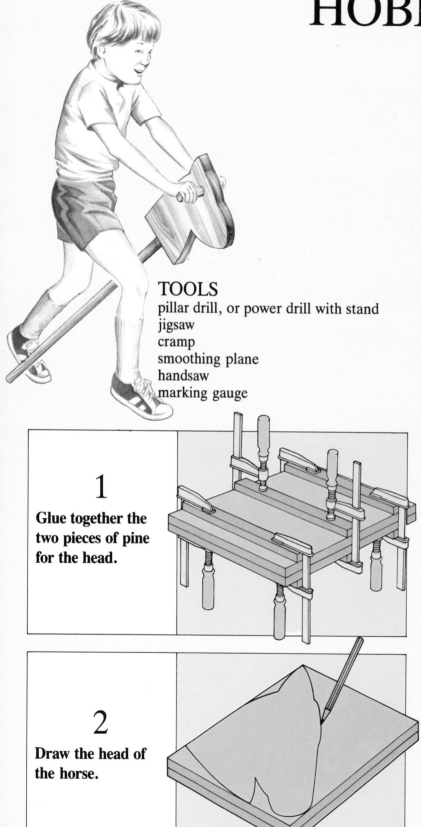

MATERIAL
pine
dowel, 21 mm (¾″) in diameter

Preparation
Start by cutting a piece of wood about 650 mm (26″) long from a pine plank, 25 × 200 mm (1″ × 8″). Secure the wood between the bench hooks and plane the heart side. First plane diagonally in both directions with the blade set coarsely (0.75–1 mm, around ¹⁄₁₆″). Check that the surface is even by placing the plane on its edge and moving it across the wood: any unevenness will show up immediately. Adjust the blade to a fine setting before finishing off along the grain.

Secure the piece of wood in such a way that an edge can be planed at right angles to the surface. Cut it in the middle with a handsaw.

TOOLS
pillar drill, or power drill with stand
jigsaw
cramp
smoothing plane
handsaw
marking gauge

1
Glue together the two pieces of pine for the head.

1
Glue the pieces together with the aid of cramps placed alternately over and under the two pieces. Make sure the planed edges are level with each other.

After the glue has dried, secure the piece of wood between the bench hooks and plane one of the surfaces until level. Turn the wood over and plane the edges. Mark the desired thickness with a marking gauge all round, and plane the workpiece to that mark.

2
Draw the head of the horse.

2
Draw the shape of the horse's head on the piece of wood. Secure with a cramp at a corner of the work bench so that most of it sticks out.

3

Cut out the shape with a jigsaw. Make sure the sole of the saw is at right angles to the blade, so that the cut is vertical.

4

Mark the holes for the crossbar (*a*) and the long pole (*b*). Define the direction of the hole for the pole by cramping two pieces of wood (*c*) on each side of the head. These pieces should be at right angles to the direction of the hole. Drill the hole in a pillar drill about 30 mm (1¼″) deep.

Drill the hole for the crossbar. To avoid splintering round the hole, drill until the point of the bit is through, then turn the wood and complete drilling from the other side.

Smooth down with coarse abrasive paper and sanding-block, including the edges, then finish off with fine paper. Always remember to sand along the grain and to round off all edges and corners.

5

Cut about 200 mm (8″) of the dowelling for the crossbar and 850 mm (34″) for the pole. Round off the ends with coarse abrasive paper and smooth both the sticks with fine paper. Glue the pole onto the head.

6

Place the crossbar in position, and mark it on each side of the head with a pencil. Then pull back the bar until both markings are visible on one side of the head. Apply glue to half the surface and knock the handle back into position.

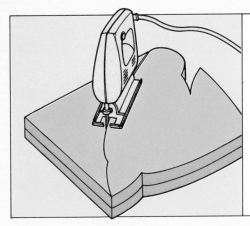

3

Cut out the head of the horse.

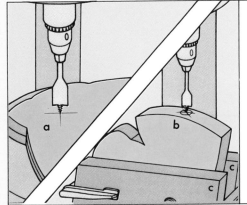

4

Drill holes for the crossbar and the pole.

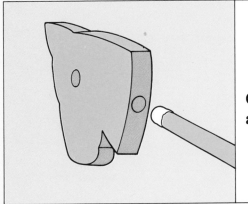

5

Cut the crossbar and pole.

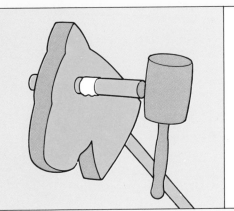

6

Glue the crossbar in position.

CARVING BOARD

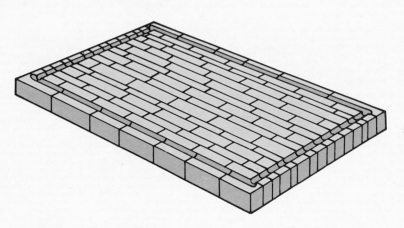

TOOLS
circular saw
handsaw
mitre box
smoothing plane
sash cramps
rasp
router

MATERIAL
off-cuts of hardwood (avoid teak which is difficult to glue because of its greasy surface)

1
Cut all the pieces to the same thickness. Use the push stick!

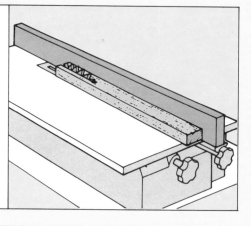

2
Glue the pieces together.

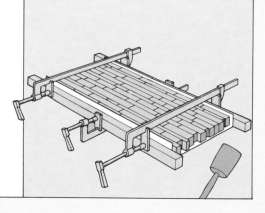

1

Cut all the pieces to the same thickness using the circular saw. The pieces can be of different widths, but the width should preferably be no greater than twice the thickness: this prevents warping if they get wet.

Cut the ends of the pieces at right angles with the aid of a mitre box. Alternatively, the circular saw and a mitre guide can be used.

2

Lay out the pieces of wood on a sheet of paper on the table in the desired pattern, being careful not to place two joints adjacent to each other. Put them between two lengths of wood cut to the required length of the carving board.

Glue the pieces of wood together. A waterproof adhesive must be used, so that the carving board can be washed. Possibilities are phenolic resin glue, which is a two-part adhesive, or polyurethane adhesive, which is a one-part adhesive. Both of them have gap-filling properties so that they fill the joint and smooth out any unevenness in the wood. The polyurethane adhesive has the added advantage of giving a clear joint.

Apply the adhesive to all the surfaces to be stuck and replace the pieces on the paper according to the pattern. Fold up the paper along the long sides of the carving board, using the two lengths of wood to hold it in place, and apply the three sash cramps sufficiently tightly to ensure adhesion.

Use a mallet to close up the pieces lengthwise, and when they are in the correct position tighten the cramps just enough for the joints to be secure. If the cramps are over-tightened, the board might bend or even spring apart.

3

Allow the adhesive to harden. Ignore excess adhesive squeezed out from joints: it will be planed away later. Trim the short ends with the handsaw or the circular saw before smoothing with the plane.

4

Plane all surfaces with the smoothing plane. The top surface should first be planed diagonally, then finished off with a series of straight strokes.

5

A draining groove is made with a router. First adjust the router fence so that the spindle will make the groove in the desired position, then start the machine and carefully guide the spindle down onto the surface of the wood. Keep it moving steadily with the fence firmly against the edges of the carving board. Avoid stopping, since the high speed of the spindle can burn the wood.

Allow the grooves of the long sides to overshoot those of the short sides slightly. This makes it easier to connect them neatly rather than attempt to make them meet exactly at right angles in the corners. Finish by lifting the spindle out of the groove.

6

Smooth all surfaces using first coarse abrasive paper, then fine. Smooth the sharp edges with the rasp.

Finishing

Since the carving board will be used for carving meat and similar things, the surface should be treated with liquid paraffin.

After washing, the surface can be kept fresh by rubbing with a slice of lemon when dry.

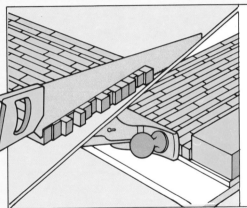

3

Saw the ends square and plane them smooth.

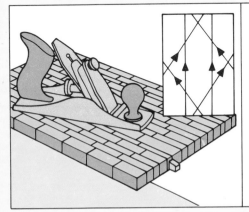

4

Plane the faces smooth.

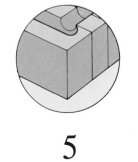

5

Rout out a groove.

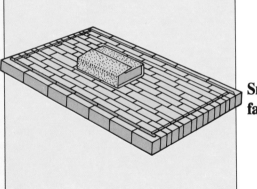

6

Smooth all the surfaces.

WORRY PUZZLE

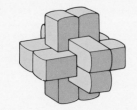

Another project that will teach you how to work in miniature. The origin of this ancient type of puzzle is unknown, but it is probably Chinese.

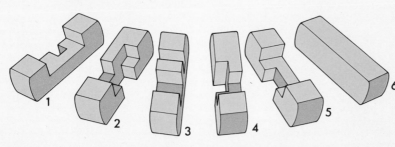

The six finished pieces of the puzzle.

MATERIAL
A hard and homogenous type of wood, such as beech, birch or maple.

TOOLS
circular saw
sanding disc

Preparation
Start by planing a length of wood 25×25 mm (1″×1″) and about one metre (39″) long. Make sure that the planed timber is square.

1

Cut six 100 mm (4″) pieces, plus a few spares.

When cutting the pieces use the rip fence (*a*) and a block of wood (*b*). Lay the block against the rip fence and adjust the fence to give the required length between the block and the saw blade. Move the block back far enough for the piece to fall free when cut off. Secure the block of wood to the rip fence with a cramp so that the standard length is maintained for the other pieces.

Hold the length of wood (*c*) against the mitre fence (*d*) and cut the pieces. To avoid splintering at the back use a wooden batten (*e*) which is slightly higher than the piece of wood being cut, and fasten it to the mitre fence with double-sided tape. Cut right into the taped batten, thus obtaining a clean cut as well as good support for each piece. Adjust the height of the blade to half the desired height, and make a trial cut. Turn the piece over and cut from the other side. Adjust till both cuts meet, and check that the cuts are right angled.

2

Fasten each piece to a longer block of wood with a small cramp, so that it can be sawn without danger.

Since the puzzle is based on whole, half and double mortises it is easiest to cut each piece in the order indicated in the picture of the finished pieces. Mark the cuts on the pieces.

Make the end cuts first, and then cut out the waste by moving the piece a blade thickness after each cut. Test a

1

Cutting each piece from the length of timber.

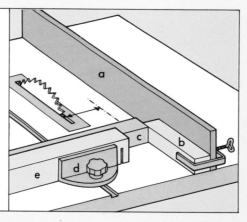

piece to ensure that the mortise is cut as accurately as possible, with no more than a tenth of 1 mm (¹⁄₁₆″) play.

3

Cut the second piece in the same way. This is the only piece that cannot be cut entirely with the circular saw: the three-quarter mortise needs trimming with a chisel. Cut 2 mm (³⁄₃₂″) from the line with a sharp chisel, and when the correct depth has been reached, trim to the line.

Continue by cutting out the other pieces, checking the fit after each one.

4

When all the pieces have been assembled, mark the ends for rounding off.

Dismantle and shape all the ends with the sanding disc. If the pieces need smoothing on the other surfaces use abrasive paper, 220 grit.

The best way of avoiding damage to edges and corners is to fasten a sheet of abrasive paper to a piece of chipboard with contact adhesive or double-sided tape, and rub the piece against the paper. Avoid rounding the edges of the interlocking surfaces, but smooth them gently with a piece of fine paper without using a block.

Finishing
Coat with liquid paraffin.

A

Place pieces 1, 2, and 3 together as in the picture and fit them together.

B

Push piece 3 as far to the right as possible without its coming completely free of the other two pieces (the dotted position in the picture). Push piece 4 through the hole that is thus created.

Drop piece 5 into place and lock the whole puzzle by pushing in piece 6.

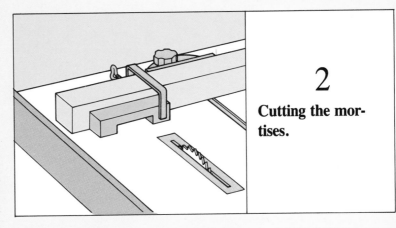

2

Cutting the mortises.

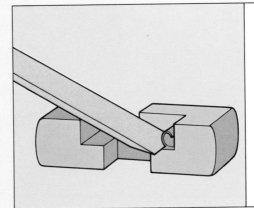

3

Use a chisel to trim the second piece.

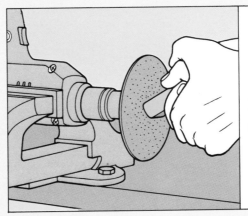

4

Round the ends of all the pieces.

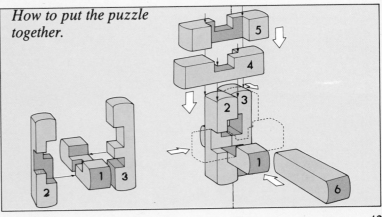

How to put the puzzle together.

PICTURE FRAME

MATERIAL
wood as preferred

TOOLS
planer
circular saw
router
tenon saw

Preparation
Cut a piece of wood twice as wide as the planned frame and slightly longer than the total length of one long side and one short.

Plane one face and one edge. Cut the wood to the correct width, and plane the cut edges of the two resultant pieces.

1

The rebate, which will hold the picture, is most easily made with the circular saw. Decide an adequate width and depth for the rebate. Set the distance between the blade and the rip fence to the desired width, and the height of the blade over the saw bench to the desired depth.

Make the cut in the wide side of each piece of wood. Then reverse the settings, so that the setting for the width becomes the depth, and vice versa. Make the second cut in the narrow side of the piece.

2

The router can be used to give the frame a decorative profile, if desired. Doing this before cutting the mitres avoids the risk of overshooting.

3

To cut the mitres, set the mitre fence of the circular saw at 45°. Make trial cuts in spare pieces of wood, checking

1

Use the circular saw for cutting a rebate in the frame pieces.

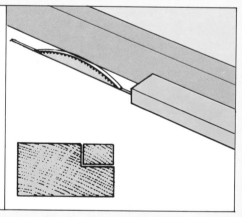

2

Make the profile of the frame with the router.

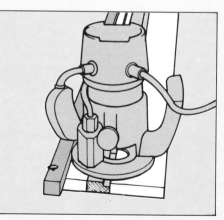

the correctness of the setting by means of a set square. The mitre cuts should be made first within the lengths of the two prepared pieces, yielding the frame's four sides with about the right lengths. Then mitre their other ends so that the opposite sides of the frame are exactly equal in length.

4

Assemble the frame and tie a piece of string to fit round it. Remove the string, apply adhesive to the mitred surfaces and roll the string back on again. Insert two blocks of wood on each side between the frame and the string, and tighten it by sliding the blocks towards the corners. Wipe off any excess adhesive.

5

Strengthen the frame by inserting tongues in the corners. Cut a piece of wood or chipboard about 150×300 mm ($6''\times12''$), and cut one short end at an angle of 45°. Adjust the rip fence so that the distance to the inner edge of the blade is equal to half the thickness of the frame.

Lean the frame against the angled support and cut the groove for the tongue in each corner. Be careful not to set the blade too high. Turn the frame around and cut once more to ensure that the groove is sufficiently wide.

6

Cut the tongues from a strip of wood, thick enough that they will fit tightly in the grooves. Glue them in position and trim with a tenon saw when the adhesive has dried. Smooth down and round off all the surfaces.

Finishing
Brush on varnish or thin transparent glaze.

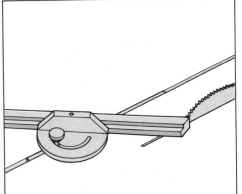

3

Cut the mitres to form the corners of the frame.

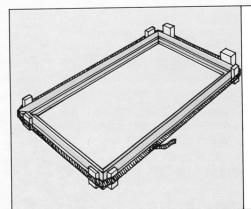

4

Glue the frame together under pressure.

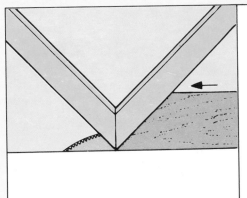

5

Cut the grooves in the corners for the reinforcing tongues, using a support piece.

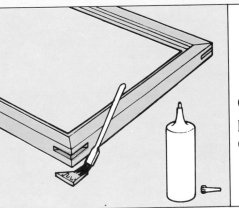

6

Glue the tongues in position and smooth down the frame.

RADIATOR COVER

TOOLS
pillar drill or
    router
planer
circular saw
cramps
stapler

MATERIAL
pine
rattan fabric

1

Cut all the pieces to form a suitable tenter frame.

1

Cut the pieces for the tenter frame. Plane the surfaces, trim the wood to the correct width and lengths, and plane the sawn surfaces.

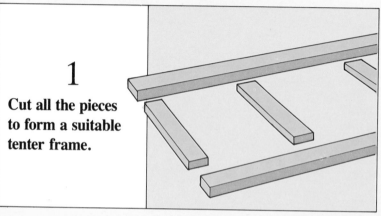

2

Mark the mortises on the long sides.

2

Mark the mortises for the tenons in the long frame pieces. The outermost mortises should be made 20 mm (⅘″) narrower than the width of the cross pieces. Note that the reduction in size is made from one direction only, and that the tenon is thus not placed centrally. The other mortises should be the same width as the cross pieces.

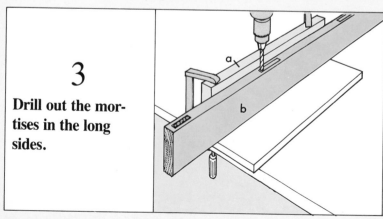

3

Drill out the mortises in the long sides.

3

Using a couple of cramps, secure a piece of wood (*a*) to the pillar drill table, so that the workpiece (*b*) can be moved to allow it to be series drilled in line.

Make the mortises by repeated drilling, then clean up with a sharp chisel.

4

Mark the tenons on the cross pieces. Set the distance between the rip fence and the outer edge of the circular saw blade to the correct tenon length, and adjust the blade height to give the required shoulder height. Cut one groove, turn the piece around and cut a groove on the other side.

Then, holding the workpiece vertical, adjust the height of the blade and the distance to the rip fence, and cut off superfluous material. The procedure must be repeated with the outermost cross pieces in order to reduce their tenon width. Remember to use a push stick!

5

Apply adhesive to the joint surfaces, fit together and secure with sash cramps.

6

Cut the rattan fabric 150 mm (6") larger than the frame on all sides. Spread it out and moisten with a damp cloth, or water it and leave for 15 minutes.

7

Place the frame on top of the fabric. Fold the overlapping edges over the frame's long sides and staple the fabric on from the middle outwards, leaving the outermost 150 mm (6") free on all sides. Cut off the superfluous fabric at the corners of the frame, fold the fabric over and staple the short sides in wrap-over fashion. Staple at 50 mm (2") intervals. Cut the fabric edges clean about 20 mm (¾") from the staples.

The outer frame is made in the same way as the picture frame on pages 44–45.

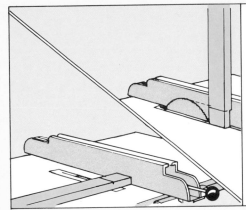

4

Cut grooves to form the tenons on the short pieces.

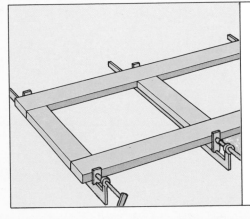

5

Glue the frame together under pressure.

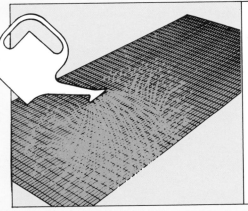

6

Water the cut-out rattan fabric so that it will dry tight.

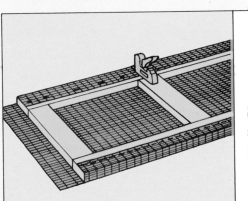

7

Secure the fabric symmetrically to the frame.

SUPPORT BRACKETS & WINDOW-LEDGE

We show here how to make sturdy brackets to support the window-ledge that is described on pages 50–51. But this type of bracket system is, if the dimensions are appropriately increased, strong enough to hold up a small cabinet, a TV shelf, or any kind of wall fixture. The connecting batten between the brackets makes the construction extra strong and provides a large fastening area, so that the system can be securely fixed to the wall.

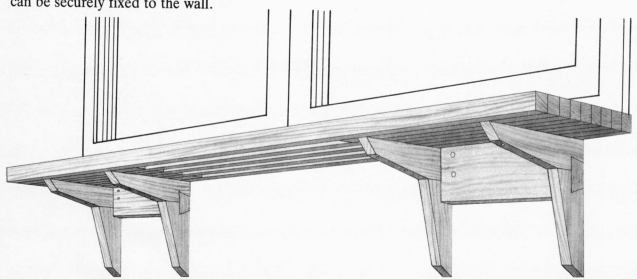

MATERIAL
pine

TOOLS
pillar drill
screw cramps
marking gauge
circular saw
tenon saw
planer/jointer
cutting snippers

The four brackets to support the window-ledge should be joined together in pairs, each bracket in a pair being fixed to one end of a connecting batten fixed to the wall.

Cut a length of board sufficient for the eight bracket parts. Plane the face side and one edge. Mark the eight wedge-shaped bracket parts on the board, cut out and plane the sawn surfaces.

1

Make mortises for the joints on four of the bracket parts with the circular saw. The mortise width should be one third of the thickness of the wood so that the brackets will have the necessary strength. Set the rip fence and make the outermost cuts, then adjust the fence slightly and make a new cut between these. Continue in this way until all the superfluous material has been removed.

2

Use the dimensions of each mortise to mark the width of the tenon on the remaining four (vertical) bracket parts. Cut out the tenon as on page 47. Glue the bracket parts together.

3

Mark the dovetail socket (*a*) about 25 mm (1″) from the upper edge of each bracket. The opening should be 35 mm (1⅜″) and the slope 10°. Mark the thickness of the connecting batten on both sides of the vertical part of the bracket with a marking gauge, to show the socket depth.

Saw down the shoulders of the dovetail socket with a tenon saw, or use the circular saw if it can be angled. Cut away the waste with a chisel. First trim to about 2 mm (¹⁄₁₆″) from the base of the socket, from both directions. Then trim along the base line, also from both directions.

4

Cut and plane the connecting batten to size. Mark the thickness of the bracket round both ends of the batten with a marking gauge.

Secure the batten with one narrow end uppermost, place the bracket on top, and mark the dovetail by tracing round the socket. Continue the lines as in the picture.

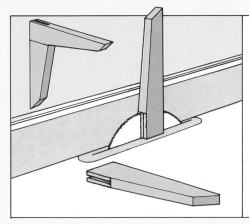

1

Cut the mortises in the four horizontal bracket parts.

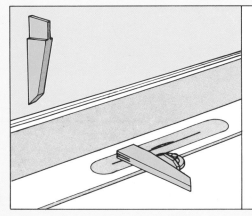

2

Cut the tenons in the four vertical bracket parts. Glue the bracket parts together.

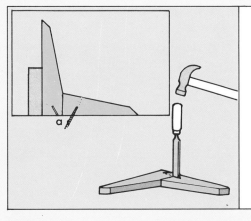

3

Cut and trim the dovetail cut-outs on the brackets.

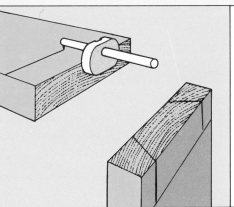

4

Cut the connecting battens to size and mark the dovetail on each narrow end.

5

Cut the tails on the connecting battens.

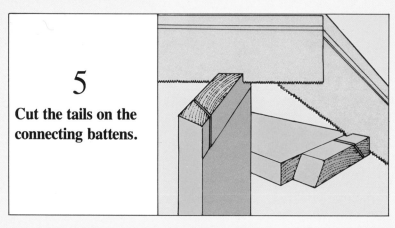

5

Cut along the angled lines on the end of the connecting batten, then lay the piece flat and cut away superfluous material. Note that when making a dovetail it is important to saw exactly on the line in order to achieve a good fit. Repeat the procedure on the batten's other end.

6

Drill the screw holes and glue the brackets to the connecting battens.

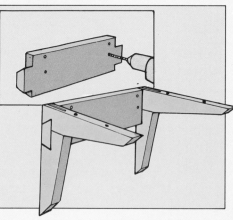

6

Drill and countersink the holes for securing the window-ledge and for screwing onto the wall. Smooth down the connecting battens and glue two brackets onto each batten.

WINDOW-LEDGE

Cut the slats for the window-ledge from a knot-free plank measuring 25×200 mm (1″×8″). Start by cutting it to length, about 40 mm (1¾″) longer than required. Now saw the plank lengthwise, plane one surface and one edge, then plane smooth on the jointer.

7

Cut the slats for the window-ledge.

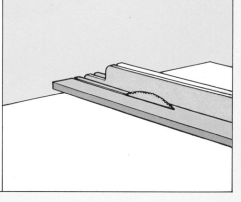

7

Decide the thickness of the slats and cut a sufficient extra number for making the spacers.

8

Cut enough spacers to give the ledge an appropriate width.

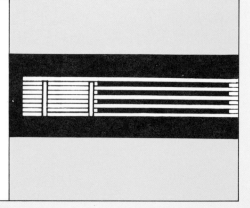

8

Decide the width of the window-ledge and estimate how many spacers are needed. Cut them from the extra slats and smooth them down lightly.

9

Glue the pieces together. Start by hammering two short brads into each spacer and snip them off to about 3 mm (⅛″) in length. Place the slats on a protective sheet and mark where the spacers are to be fastened. Apply adhesive to both sides of the spacers and place them in position between the slats. Place a couple of pieces of wood on each side and cramp together lightly with sash cramps. The snipped-off brads will prevent the spacers from sliding lengthwise.

   Place pieces of wood above and below so that screw cramps can be secured vertically. Then tighten all cramps until the joints are firm.

10

Plane and cut to size. Smooth down and round off edges and corners.

11

Treat the surface with linseed or paraffin oil. (Boiled linseed oil should be mixed with 30% white spirit or turpentine. Remember it is inflammable, and so soak all cloths and paper in water.)

   Alternatively, sand down and apply several coats of varnish. Add a little white paint to the varnish to counteract the action of the sunlight.

12

Place the window-ledge in position. First screw the brackets' connecting battens onto the wall, then screw on the ledge.

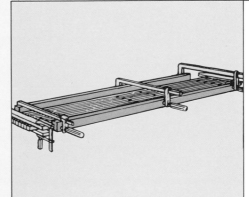

9

Glue together the spacers and the slats.

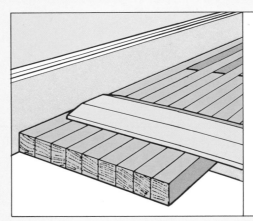

10

Plane the window-ledge and cut to the desired length.

11

Treat the surface. Remember the fire risk of oily rags or paper.

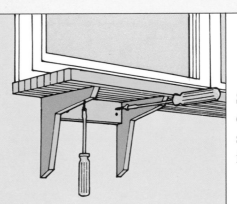

12

Screw on the window-ledge. Use a spirit level to ensure it is horizontal.

TOOL BOX

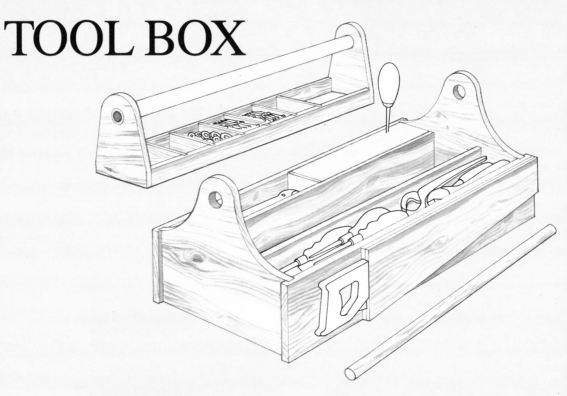

MATERIAL
12 mm (½″) plywood
dowel 25 mm (1″) in diameter
plastic tubing
3 mm (⅛″) hardboard or plywood
polystyrene foam
rectangular softwood moulding

TOOLS
circular saw
coping saw or jigsaw
router
drill with 25 mm (1″) bit
sash cramps

This box consists of three longitudinal sections, an insert tray, and a side compartment for a handsaw. The length of the box depends on that of the handsaw. The width depends on your hand, and how much room is needed to get hold of things inside. The height should be equal to your longest screwdriver.

Mark the parts on the sheet of plywood so that they can be cut out in strips. Cut the bottom and ends from the same strip, for instance.

1

Cut the sides (*a*), bottom (*b*) and ends (*c*).

Make grooves (*d*) in the sides for the ends with a 12 mm (½″) rebating cutter. The grooves should be about 4 mm (⁵⁄₃₂″) deep and about 10 mm (⅜″) from the edge.

Make grooves (*e*) in the sides and ends with the same setting for fixing the bottom. N.B.: These grooves should not overshoot the ones made for fixing the ends to the sides.

Make grooves (*f*) in the ends to hold

1

Mark and cut the various parts, and cut out the fixing grooves.

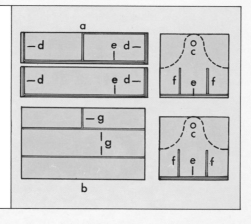

the dividers. The length of the grooves should be equal to the height of the sides.

Mark the three grooves (g) where the dividers are to be fixed to the bottom.

2

Cramp a batten (a) to the bottom (b). The batten serves as a guide for the router when making the grooves, which should be 4 mm (5/32″) deep.

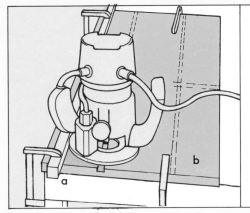

2

Cut the grooves for the dividers in the bottom piece.

3

Cut a piece of 12 mm (½″) plywood for the dividers. The width should be twice the inside height of the box plus 8 mm (5/16″) – for the routed grooves – plus 2 mm (3/32″) – for the width of the saw blade.

Cut the piece to equal the inside measurement of the box plus a fraction less than 8 mm (5/16″) – to allow for the glue. Cut in two lengthwise.

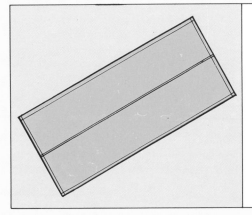

3

Mark and cut the dividers.

4

One of the side compartments should be subdivided.

Place one side (a) and one divider (b) side by side so that the distance from the end of the side to the end of the divider is equal at both ends. Mark the groove (c) for the dividing wall on both pieces and cut it with the router.

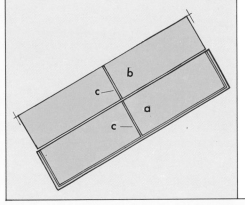

4

Mark and cut the groove for the dividing wall in one of the side compartments.

5

Cut the outline of the ends with the coping saw or jigsaw, and drill the holes for the handle. Cut two pieces of rectangular batten (a) as rests for the insert tray. Pre-drill and countersink. Screw in position.

Smooth the insides with abrasive paper and glue together the sides, partitions and bottom using sash cramps or 25 mm (1″) brads.

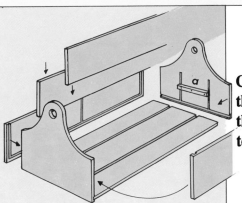

5

Cut the outline of the ends and glue the tool box together.

6

Measure and cut the parts of the insert tray. Cut the grooves for the partitions.

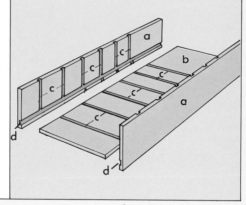

6

The insert tray is made from a long piece of 12 mm (½") plywood, the width of which is equal to two sides (a) plus the bottom (b) plus twice the width of the circular-saw blade.

Cut the piece so that its length equals the inside measurement of the tray less 19 mm (¾"). In other words, the length is reduced by twice the thickness of the tray end minus the depth of the groove. That is, 2×[12–4]

mm=16 mm, or 2×[¾"–5/32"]=11/16", and then a further 3 mm (⅛") is subtracted to allow for free movement of the insert tray. The total length has thus been reduced by 19 mm (¾").

Mark grooves (c) for partitions in the tray. They should be made of 3 mm (⅛") hardboard or plywood. Cut out the grooves with the saw blade set to a depth of 4 mm (5/32"). Since the saw blade is about 2 mm (3/32") thick, you will have to saw twice.

Cut the piece into three strips, i.e. two sides and the bottom.

Make grooves (d) for the bottom in both side pieces.

7

Make the ends of the insert tray and drill holes for its handle. Cut the grooves for the ends. Glue together.

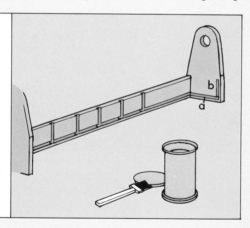

7

Cut two pieces of 12 mm (½") plywood for the ends of the insert tray. They should be 60 mm (2½") shorter than the box ends and about 2 mm (3/32") narrower than the middle section of the box.

Mark the curve of the box ends on the ends of the insert tray and cut.

Drill holes for the handle in the ends. The diameter should be the same as that of the plastic tubing.

Mark a 12 mm (½") groove (a) for the bottom of the deck. This can be made with the circular saw.

Make grooves (b) for the sides.

Smooth the insides with abrasive paper and glue the pieces of the insert tray together. Reinforce with 25 mm (1") brads.

8

Cut the partitions of the insert tray, and glue them in place.

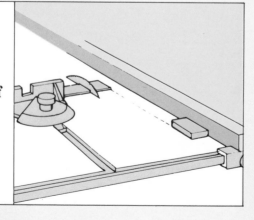

8

Cut a piece of 3 mm (⅛") plywood or hardboard with the circular saw for the partitions of the insert tray. The width should equal the inside measurements of the tray plus twice the depth of the grooves.

Cut the partitions to size in the circular saw. To prevent the pieces being thrown back, use a spacing block to set the measurement (see page 42).

9

Cut two pieces of moulding (a) 2 mm (3/32") wider than half the thickness of the handle of the handsaw. Place the handsaw in position, and fasten the mouldings above and below the saw with glue and pins. Cut a piece of plywood (b) as a lid, and glue and pin it in place.

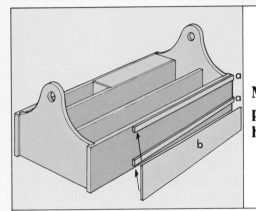

9

Make the side compartment for the handsaw.

10

Cut the dowel (a) a little longer than the box so that it will not slide out of position when the tool box is carried.

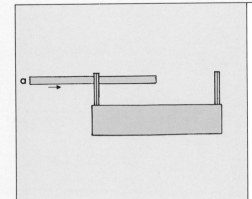

10

Cut dowelling for the handle of the tool box.

11

Cut the polystyrene foam so that it fills the space for chisels and screwdrivers. The foam keeps the tools in place and protects the edges.

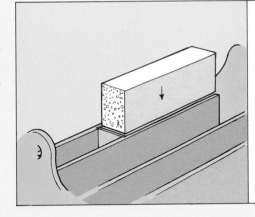

11

Fill the compartment for chisels and screwdrivers with polystyrene foam.

12

Cut a piece of hard plastic tubing to form the handle of the insert tray. The tubing should have a slightly larger diameter than the main handle so that the dowelling fits into the plastic tube when the box is assembled. Glue the tube in place with phenolic resin glue.

Finishing
Sand down and varnish.

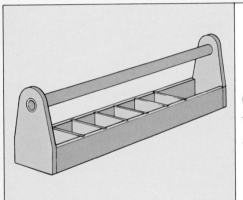

12

Cut the handle of the insert tray and assemble it.

STORAGE BOX

The joint used here is the classic box joint, also known as the finger joint or the comb joint. The great number of pins, or fingers, increases the contact surface of the joint, so that it is very strong when glued. In addition, the two parts lock together vertically.

1

The picture shows the circular saw from above, with a jig which increases the speed and efficiency with which the pins and sockets can be made. It is made of two slats (*a*) and (*b*), fastened to the mitre fence (*c*) of the circular saw with two screws. A bolt (*d*) with a wing-nut holds the two slats together.

MATERIAL
hardwood or pine for the sides
fibreboard or plywood for the bottom

TOOLS
circular saw
router

2

Shown here at top is a front view of the jig. To enable the saw blade to run freely, slat (*a*) needs a cut (*e*). The other slat (*b*) needs a slit (*f*) so that it can be moved to adjust the positions of the various fingers. The cut is best made with the circular saw, and the slit with the router. Then drill a hole (*g*) for the bolt to hold the slats together.

The turnable heel (*h*) is set into the slat (*b*), as shown in the two views from above. The heel is attached to the slat with a screw so that it can be turned; one of its corners has been rounded. With the piece of wood pressed against the heel in position 1, the saw cuts the "base measure". When the heel is in position 2, it extends the slat by the width of a saw cut, so that the saw cuts the "base measure" plus the width of the cut. If a circular saw is used with a wobbling blade, the heel should still extend the slat by the width of the saw cut.

3

Cut the box sides to the required lengths, and number the ends.

4

Mark out the fingers on one of the ends. All the fingers and sockets should be equal in width and the joints should be symmetrical.

The procedure for marking is as follows. If you want a finger outermost at each side, an odd number of divisions, 7 for example, is needed. Place a ruler diagonally over the wood so that its measurement is divisible by seven. If the measure is, say, 14, marks should be made at 2, 4, 6, 8, 10, and 12. Draw lines through these points parallel to the edges of the piece of wood and the end will be divided into seven exactly identical parts (measure *x*). The thickness of the wood gives us the measure *y*.

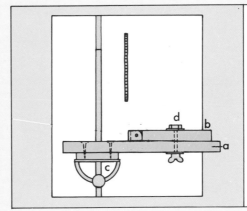

1

Plan view of the jig for making the fingers and sockets.

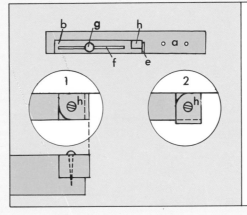

2

The parts of the jig, with the heel in its two positions.

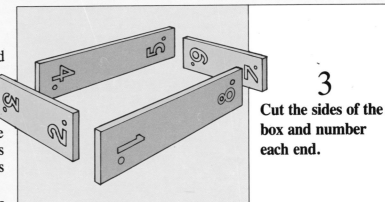

3

Cut the sides of the box and number each end.

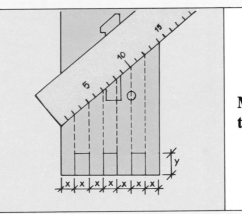

4

Mark up the tongues and sockets.

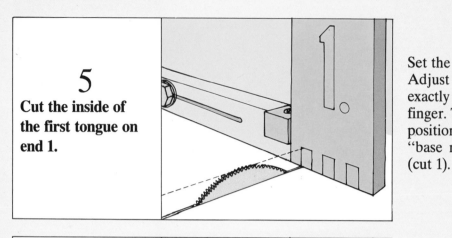

5

Cut the inside of the first tongue on end 1.

5

Set the blade for the cut to be *y* high. Adjust the jig so that the blade cuts exactly against the inside of the first finger. The heel of the jig should be in position 1, i.e. the jig should have its "base measure". Make the first cut (cut 1).

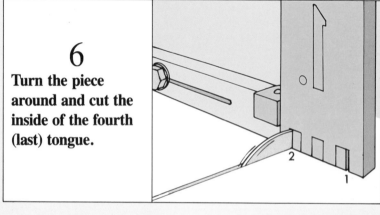

6

Turn the piece around and cut the inside of the fourth (last) tongue.

6

Turn the piece of wood around and make the next cut (cut 2) with the jig on the same setting.

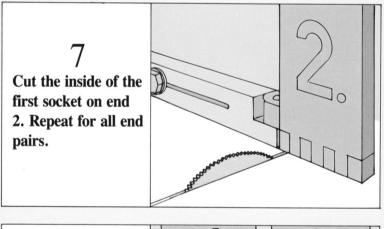

7

Cut the inside of the first socket on end 2. Repeat for all end pairs.

7

Without changing the setting of the blade or the "base measure" of the jig, continue with end two. It should interlock with end one: where end one has a finger, end two should have a socket. To achieve this, the setting of the jig must be adjusted so that the blade cuts against the outside of the first finger of end two, making cut 1 for end two. Adjust the setting by turning the heel into position 2.

The piece of wood has thus been moved the width of a saw cut in relation to the blade. Repeat the procedure as for end one (see step 6), and continue in the same way for the other corners of the box.

8

Continue for the other fingers and sockets on all the end pairs.

8

Having adjusted the basic setting of the jig, continue making the other cuts, using the same method for cuts 3 and 4, then 5 and 6, on all the ends.

9

After all the basic cuts have been made, the sockets are cut clean. Move the workpiece by the width of the saw blade, cut by cut.

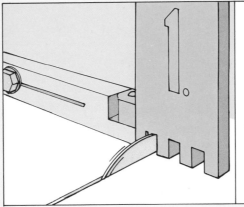

9
Cut the fingers and sockets clean with the circular saw.

10

To give the bottom of the box a secure base, make grooves on the insides of the side pieces so that a sheet of fibreboard or plywood can be slid in. The groove is best made with a router (see picture). If a circular saw is used, it will go through the corners of the box and leave ugly holes.

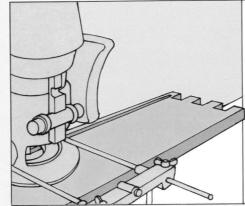

10
Rout out the grooves in the sides for the bottom.

11

After the bottom has been placed in position, the box can be glued together. Use wood adhesive for the joints; the bottom of the box needs no gluing.

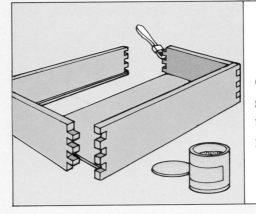

11
Glue two adjoining sides, insert the bottom, glue the remaining sides.

12

After the box has been assembled, the joints can be pressed together with the aid of strap cramps or a piece of string tied round the box. Cut eight wooden wedges and slide them between the straps and the box, one at each side of each corner, to tighten the straps.

Finishing
Varnishing is the best finishing treatment.

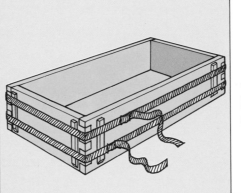

12
Allow to dry under pressure from strap cramps and blocks.

COFFEE TABLE

MATERIAL
boards of pine or hardwood
6 mm (¼") plywood for tongues

TOOLS
planer
circular saw
pillar drill
sanding machine
router
tenon saw
smoothing plane
sash cramps
bevel gauge

The measurements given on the illustration may not suit you. When you plan your own coffee table and make the drawing, you should take into account the measurements of your sofa or of the chairs that will be placed around the table.

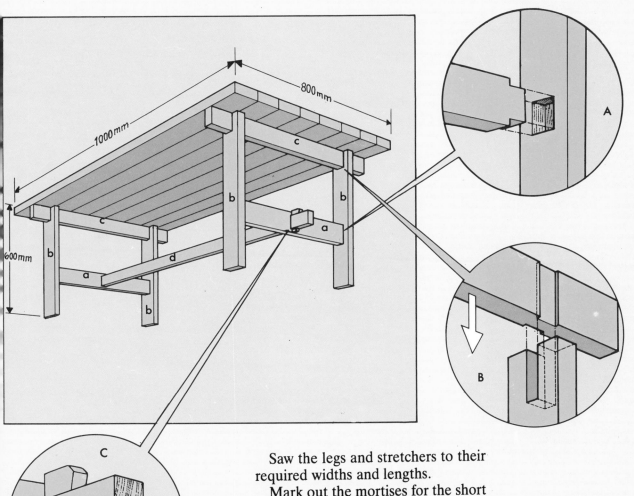

Saw the legs and stretchers to their required widths and lengths.

Mark out the mortises for the short stretchers (a) on the legs (b) — see fig. A — and the bridle joints for the supports (c) at the tops of the legs — see fig. B. The open mortises for the supports are made 6 mm (¼″) narrower than the thickness of the supports. The mortises for the short stretchers are the same thickness as the stretchers, but 20 mm (¾″) less in height.

Mark out the mortises for the long stretcher (d) in the short stretchers — see fig. C. They should be the same thickness as the long stretcher, but 30 mm (1³⁄₁₆″) less than its height. Mark out on both sides of the respective pieces.

LEGS AND FRAME
Preparation
Cut all parts about 20 mm (¾″) longer than the final measurements required.

Use the planer to smooth one face and one edge on all the pieces. Then plane the remaining surfaces to the required thickness.

## 1 **Drill around the mortise lines on each leg.**	

Joint A

1

Cut the mortises for the short stretchers in the legs (*a*), using the pillar drill. Start drilling at the ends of the area marked out, then drill in between. Fit the drill with a suitable depth stop, or set the stop on the drill stand, so as not to drill right through the wood.

2

Use a chisel to clean out the mortise.

2

Clean out the mortise with a chisel. Start chiselling a little way short of the marked mortise lines, so that you can then work accurately up to them.

3

Mark up the tenons and saw their length on the short stretchers. Don't saw too deep!

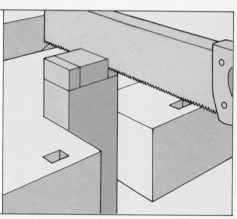

3

Saw the tenon to the correct thickness with the tenon saw. First make a very small cut. Then turn the wood and make a correspondingly small cut on the other side. Check that these cuts will exactly match the mortises you have cut in the legs. Then saw down to the shoulder.

4

Saw off the waste on the short stretchers.

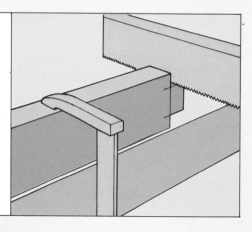

4

Saw off the waste material with the tenon saw. Alternatively, cut out the tenons on the circular saw, as on page 47.

Joint B

5

Mark out the tenons on the supports (*a*) and cut them with the circular saw. Set the blade to correspond to the depth of the tenon's shoulder. Start at the outer edge of your marks, then saw out the waste material in between by moving the workpiece over the blade several times, supported by the mitre fence.

For fastening the table top to the supports, four 6 mm (¼″) screw holes are to be drilled at even intervals along the supports. All but 25 mm (1″) of each hole is counterbored with a 12 mm (½″) drill so that the screwheads are recessed.

6

Check that the markings for the open mortise of the tops of the legs correspond with the tenons cut in the supports. Cut out the waste material in the tops of the legs, using the tenon saw and a chisel.

7

Start cutting with the chisel about 2 mm (1/16″) from the line that marks the bottom of the open mortise. Cut away about half of the waste material, but don't cut out as far as the edge. Turn the leg over and repeat, until the remaining waste falls off.

8

Square off the bottom of the open mortise.

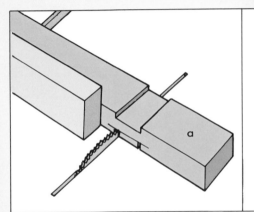

5

Mark up and saw out the tenons on the supports.

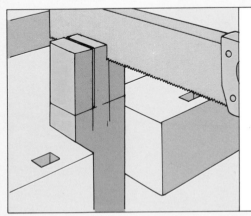

6

Saw down the marked lines for the open mortise.

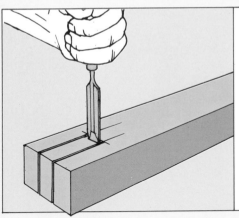

7

Use the chisel to cut away waste. Work from both sides.

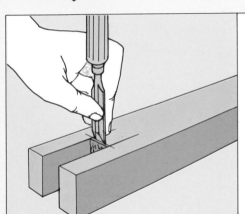

8

Make sure the bottom of the open mortise is square.

Joint C (between the long and short stretchers)

Preparation

Cut the marked mortises with the pillar drill in the short stretcher, as you did for joint A. Do not drill straight through the wood, but turn the pieces over after the hole is started and drill out the rest from the opposite direction. In this way, you will avoid splintering when the drill breaks through.

9

Make holes in the long stretcher for the wedges.

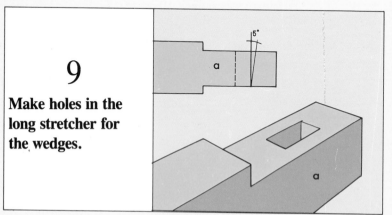

In the long stretcher (*a*) mark out the holes for the wedges. These should not exceed one-third of the thickness of the long stretcher. Drill out the holes—working from both sides—on the pillar drill. Next, make the holes vertical on the inner side towards the short stretcher, and angled (maximum 5°) on the outer side (use a chisel and bevel gauge).

Saw off all faces, and round off all edges, except for the top surface of the supports, using rough abrasive paper.

ASSEMBLING THE UNDERFRAME

10

Check that each set of legs is in true. Glue each set.

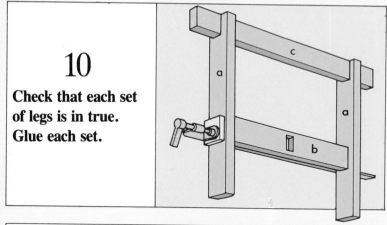

Fit together the two sections comprising the legs (*a*), the short stretchers (*b*) and the supports (*c*), without gluing. Check that the assembled parts are square and straight. If they are out of true, shave wood off the tenons on the short stretchers with a chisel to adjust their angle.

Leaving the supports in place to keep each set of legs true, glue together the legs and the short stretchers. Use sash cramps and cushion blocks. Wipe away any excess glue with a piece of wet rag.

11

Prepare the wedges with a plane.

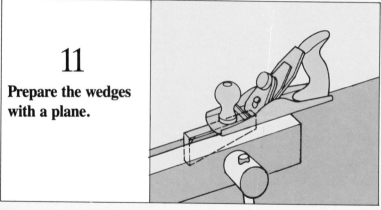

Cut the wedges, form them with the smoothing plane, and adjust their tapering with abrasive paper.

12

Fit the long stretcher into the short ones, and knock the wedges into place.

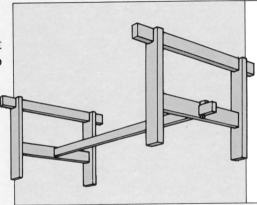

12

Fit the long stretcher in place. Insert its wedges.

THE TABLE TOP

13

Cut the lengths of wood about 30 mm (1³⁄₁₆″) longer than the required length of the table top. Rip saw each piece in two equal widths along its entire length. The resulting planks, being narrower, will not distort or cup.

In the planer, smooth one side and one edge of each length. Check that the two faces are at right angles, then plane the other two faces. If you find it difficult to get an exact right angle, plane each two adjoining edges together, so that even if the edges are not precisely at right angles the match is still perfect (see picture and inset).

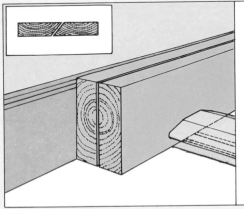

13

Prepare the pieces for the table top.

14

Arrange the lengths of wood in their final pattern on a pair of saw horses. Lay them the same way up, heartwood with heartwood and sapwood with sapwood. Then number them in order.

Test the assembled table top by lightly tensioning a pair of sash cramps and checking that all the joints are flush. If necessary, correct a piece by dismantling it and feeding it through the jointer, which is set to make its very finest cut.

14

Lay them out in pattern. DON'T put heartwood against sapwood. Heartwood always against heartwood, sapwood against sapwood.

15

The simplest method of joining is to butt-joint the lengths of wood, gluing them edge to edge.

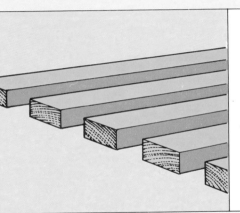

15

Alternative 1: butt-jointing.

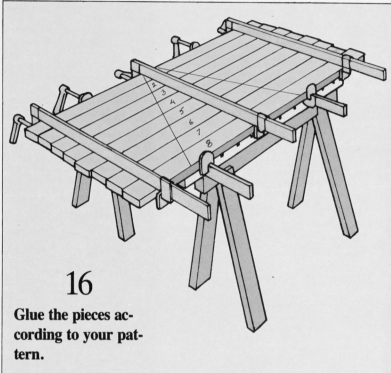

16

Glue the pieces according to your pattern.

16

Set out your sash cramps, glue, and glue brush: it is important to have all your tools to hand, as you have only 2–3 minutes to assemble all the components after you have applied the glue. If the temperature is high, then this time will be even shorter.

Arrange the lengths of wood in their numerical order and then stand all of them — except the last one — together on their sides. Brush on the glue, lay down the pieces again and press together with sash cramps.

Place the sash cramps along the length of the table top and tighten, beginning from the centre (see picture). Arrange them alternately above and below the table top so that it does not bend. Tighten the cramps, checking that the top stays flat. Use a wet rag to remove any glue that has been squeezed out.

17

Alternative 2: blind tongue-and-groove joints.

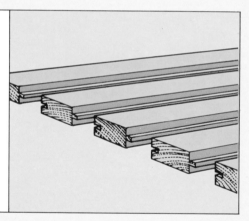

17

If you have a spindle moulder available, you can make blind tongue-and-groove joints on the lengths of wood that will make up the table top. Glue as for butt-jointing.

18

Alternative 3: loose tongue-and-groove joints.

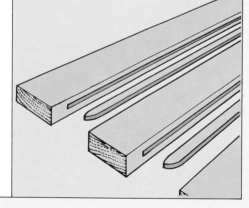

18

If you have no spindle moulder, a router can be used to make loose tongue-and-groove joints. (You can also do this with the circular saw, if you do not mind the joints showing at the ends of the table top.)

The grooves should be about 8 mm (5⁄16″) deep and the thickness of the plywood in width. Cut all the grooves working from the same side, to avoid twisting the tongues.

Saw the strips of plywood for the tongues. They should be at least 1 mm narrower than the combined depth of the grooves. Trim then in the planer so that they fit. Note: they will swell after gluing and therefore should not fit too tightly.

Glue as for butt-jointing, but the tongues need to have glue brushed on before they are inserted in their grooves.

19

When the glue is completely dry, cut the table top to the required length with the circular saw or a handsaw.

Smooth the edges in the planer. Plane about 30 mm (1³⁄₁₆″) from one direction, turn the top and then plane the whole edge. This reduces the risk of splintering the ends.

20

Sand down the surfaces and edges with a sanding machine, at the same time rounding off all sharp corners and edges.

21

Screw the supports to the table top.

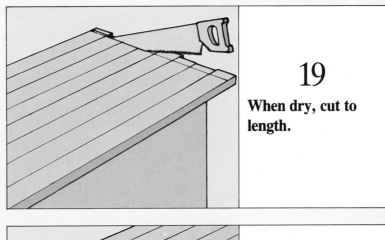

19

When dry, cut to length.

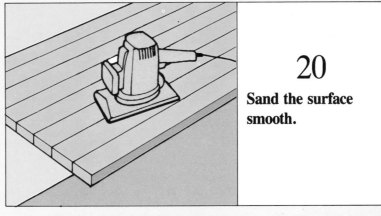

20

Sand the surface smooth.

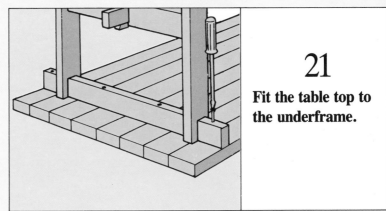

21

Fit the table top to the underframe.

Finishing

The type of finish you select depends both on the material and on the intended use of the table. If you have chosen a softwood, such as pine, you will have to give it a protective coat of two-component lacquer after rubbing it down with fine-grade abrasive paper.

However, if you have picked a harder type of wood, such as ash or oak, you can preserve as much as poss-ible of its character and "feel" by simply oiling or waxing the surface, after rubbing it down well with fine-grade abrasive paper. But if there are children in the family, you should consider whether a protective coat of two-component lacquer might not be preferable. Otherwise children's paints, felt pens, etc., may force you to be forever renovating the table surface.

PANELLED DOORS

MATERIAL
softwood or hardwood (should be dry
     and knot-free)
plywood (optional)

TOOLS
circular saw
planer
smoothing plane
router with rebating cutter

1

First, decide the width of the pieces
for the door frame, and the combined
length of one stile (long side) and one
rail (short side). Choose a board twice
as wide as one of the door frame
pieces, and longer than the combined
length—by about 5 cm (2″).

    Plane both faces and one edge. Rip-
cut the board with the circular saw,
and plane the sawn edges.

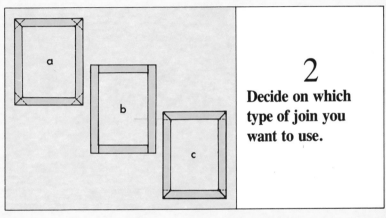

1

**Prepare the parts of
the frame from one
board.**

2

Decide what method of jointing you
want to use: (*a*) tongued (keyed)
mitre, (*b*) mortise and tenon, or (*c*)
mitred bridle joint. The last two give
the strongest joint.

2

**Decide on which
type of join you
want to use.**

3 **Cut the workpieces to rough length.**	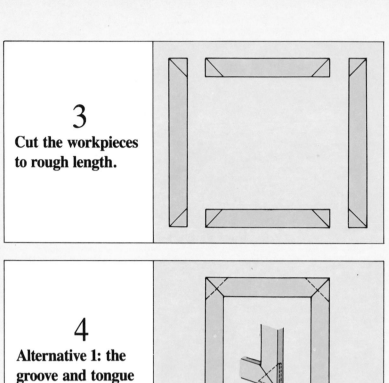

3

Cut the planed board into pieces for the frame: two stiles (that is, the long sides of the frame), one bottom rail, and one top rail. Remember to allow extra for the fact that the pieces are going to be jointed.

4 **Alternative 1: the groove and tongue mitre.**	

4

For mitring with tongues, cut the mitres on the four frame pieces, glue together, and then cut the grooves for the tongues, as is done with the picture frame (pages 44–45).

5 **Alternative 2: mortise and tenon joint.**	

5

For the mortise and tenon joint, proceed as with the frame for the radiator cover (pages 46–47). Note that the tenons must be at least 15 mm (⅝″) in from the frame's edges, to avoid breaking through them when cutting the rebate later.

6 **Alternative 3: the bridled joint.**	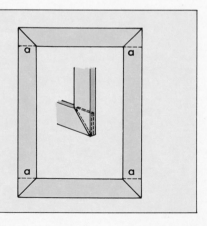

6

The method of joining with mitred bridles also has the advantage that you can rout a decorative profile before gluing. This is the method shown here.

First, mark the rail width (*a*) on the edge of each stile, measuring from each end of it, to show where the rails will join it.

7

Next, divide the end of each stile into three equal parts. Adjust the rip fence of the circular saw so that its distance from the blade's inner face equals one of these parts. Adjust the saw blade to a height that equals the rail width.

Now make the bridle mortise in the ends of each stile. Saw in one direction, then turn the end round to saw in the other direction. Clean out the mortise with intermediate cuts, moving the rip fence by one blade width at a time.

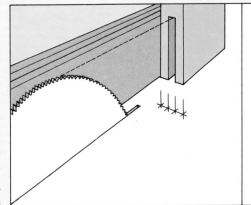

7

Saw out the bridle in the stile ends.

8

Adjust the mitre fence of the circular saw to 45°, and cut a mitre in each of the stile ends.

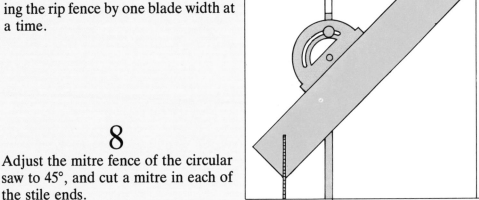

8

Now make mitres in the stile ends.

9

Cut the rails to their exact lengths, x, plus twice the width of the stiles (for the mitres). Cut a 45° mitre in each end.

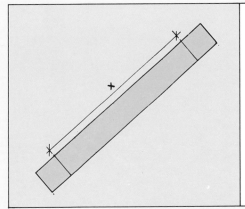

9

Cut the rails to their exact lengths.

10

Find out the correct thickness for the tenons by making a test-piece (*a*) that fits exactly into the bridle mortises. Then use the circular saw to make two cuts, separated by that thickness, in each end of each rail. The saw blade's height must equal the diagonal (*y*), which you measure. Saw the vertical (long) cuts for the tenons.

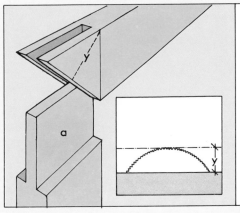

10

Measure the thickness of the tenons.

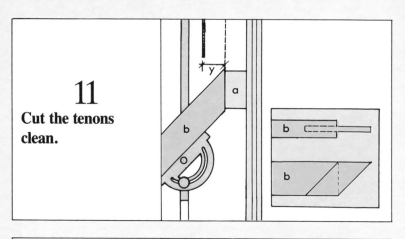

11
Cut the tenons clean.

11

To cut the tenons clean, place a block (*a*) against the rip fence, at the distance (*y*) from the saw blade's outer edge. Adjust the blade to a height of one third of a rail thickness. Lay each rail (*b*) flush with the distancing block and the mitre fence.

Remove the block and push the rail to cut it. Then turn it over and cut its opposite face similarly, rotating the mitre fence by 90° to hold it. Finally, cut off the tenons' pointed ends at a right angle (the dotted line in the lower of the inset drawings).

12
Glue the door frame together.

12

Assemble the rails and stiles and glue the frame together, using wood adhesive and string or band cramps.

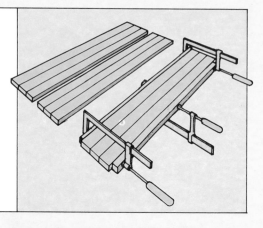

13
Prepare and glue together the door panel.

13

To make the door panel, saw pieces at most 75 mm (3″) wide, from a board 19 mm (¾″) thick. Plane their surfaces and edges. Lay the pieces in a suitable pattern and mark them.

Glue the pieces together as for the coffee table (pages 65–67), then plane again. If the plane is not wide enough, glue smaller sections and plane them separately before joining them.

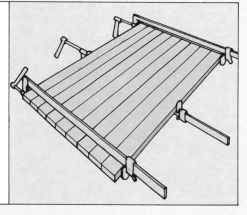

14
Plane and cut the panel to size.

14

Once the whole panel is glued together with sash cramps, any uneven areas can be removed with a smoothing plane.

Plane one edge and cut the panel to the correct width, using the circular saw. Cut one short side squarely, measure the correct panel height from there, subtract 1 mm (¹⁄₃₂″), and cut the other short side.

15

The router or saw can be used to cut a profile on the panel faces.

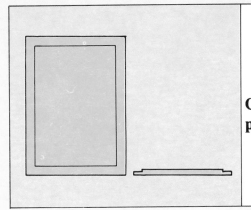

15
Cut a profile on the panel face.

16

Now cut the grooves to hold the panel, using the router with a rebating cutter with guide. Chisel out the corners. If the panel is solid wood, it needs at least 2 mm (⅛″) expansion room on each vertical side.

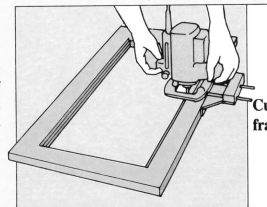

16
Cut grooves in the frame for the panel.

17

Lay the panel in place, and measure a suitable thickness for the mounting strips or beads. They can be slightly thicker than the groove depth.

Saw out the strips and smooth them down. Fix them over the panel edges with small panel pins.

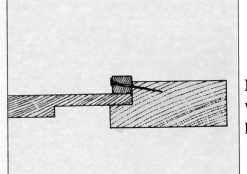

17
Mount the panel with beading and panel pins.

18

A simpler panel can be made from an ordinary plywood sheet, which is mounted in much the same way.

18
Alternative panel. Use a plywood sheet.

Finishing
Smooth down the entire door and treat the surface as desired.

VENEERED TRINKET BOX

MATERIAL
beech, birch or ash veneer
piece of wood, of same type as the
   veneer
any type of wood to use for a
   mould
adhesive (phenolic resin or
   polyurethane)

TOOLS
planer
circular saw
bandsaw
smoothing plane
handsaw
veneer saw
steel rule or straight edge
elastic bands
marking gauge
strap clamps

1

Start by making a mould around which the box will be built up. Plane the face-side of a suitable length of 50 mm (2") wood, cut it in the middle with the handsaw, and glue the pieces together.

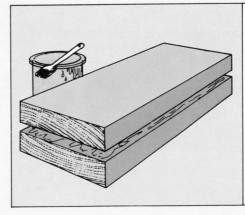

1

Glue two pieces together to form the workpiece.

2

When it has dried, plane the glued timber all round. Draw a line down the centre and mark the length of the box on the line; 250 mm (10") might be considered suitable. Mark a point on the centre line 50 mm (2") from each end of the box. Hammer a pin into each of these points, and attach a piece of string running from one pin (*a*), past the second pin (*b*) to the outer marking (*c*) and back to the second pin (*b*). Place a pencil inside the string, stretch tightly and draw an ellipse on the wood.

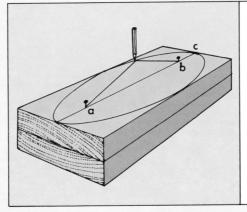

2

Mark up the trinket box's oval shape.

3

Cut with the bandsaw and smooth down any unevenness.

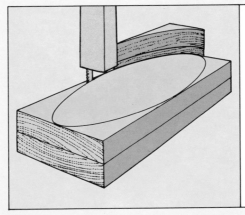

3

Cut out the shape on the bandsaw.

4

Start by giving the veneer a straight edge, using the veneer saw and the steel rule. Regarding this straight edge as the bottom border of the box, mark the height of the box (the broken line) on the veneer and cut it out.

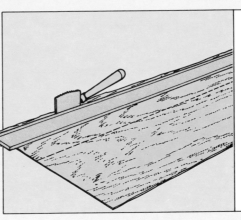

4

Cut out strips on veneer with the veneer saw.

5
Wind the veneer around the mould.

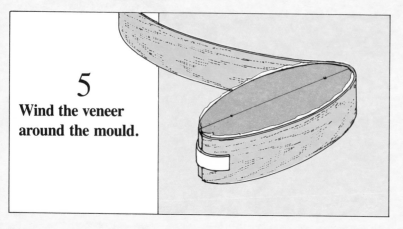

5

Fasten a piece of paper around the mould with tape. Apply adhesive to one side of the veneer, and tape one end of it onto the paper. Start rolling the veneer around the mould.

Use rubber gloves or disposable gloves to protect your hands. Any glue coming into contact with the skin must be removed quickly with thinner and soap and water.

6
Secure the veneer with bands while it is drying.

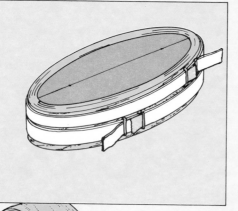

6

Continue by rolling on as many layers of veneer as necessary to achieve the required thickness, then hold the veneer in place with strap clamps.

7
Trim the edges and smooth the insides.

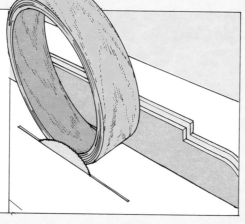

7

When the glue has dried, remove the mould and smooth down one edge of the "veneer tube" with a smoothing plane, then cut the other edge parallel with the circular saw. Smooth down the inside of the box, paying special attention to the joint where the first veneer end was stuck on.

8
Make the workpiece for the lid and bottom.

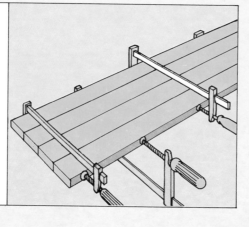

8

Cut strips from the piece of wood intended for the lid and the bottom. The strips should be 65 mm (2⁹⁄₁₆″) wide and 13 mm (½″) thick. They are glued together to form a piece large enough for the lid and bottom twice over.

9

When the glue has dried, plane the piece to a thickness of 11 mm (just over

⅜"), then draw the inside contour of the box onto it twice. Also draw two contours which are the thickness of the veneer wall wider. Cut out these four pieces with the bandsaw. Smooth down with abrasive paper so that the part intended for the bottom of the box fits tightly while the lid part fits loosely.

10

Mark where the inside pieces of the lid and the bottom should be glued on to the outside pieces. Face-side should be glued to face-side.

Hammer a couple of brads into the inside pieces to make sure there is no movement when gluing. Use lengths of wood and cramps to assist the gluing process.

11

When the glue has dried, smooth down the edge of the lid and the bottom, and slightly round off the bottom edges.

Mark a line on the lid top with the marking gauge 30 mm (1⅛") from the edge, and another line about 4 mm (5/32") down the edge. Then round off with a smoothing plane between the lines, working from the first line towards the edge. Smooth down with coarse abrasive paper and finish off along the grain with fine abrasive paper.

12

Glue the bottom onto the box. Smooth down the outside, especially where the last veneer end was glued on. Round off the upper edge of the box slightly. The top can be provided with a handle or knob.

Finishing

Use oil or a thin layer of varnish. When dry, the wood will have swollen a little. Smooth down the surface with fine steel wool until it is soft and smooth.

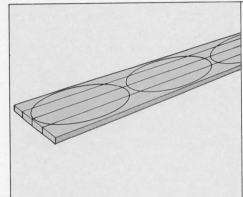

9

Plane the workpiece and mark up the inside contours.

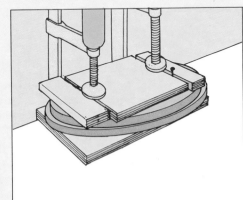

10

Glue the two lid pieces together. Same for the bottom.

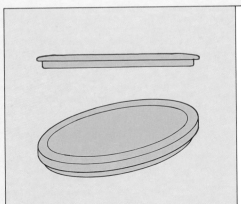

11

Bevel the edges and smooth off.

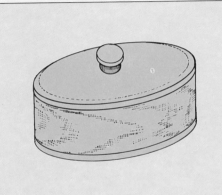

12

Glue the bottom to the box. Attach a knob to the lid.

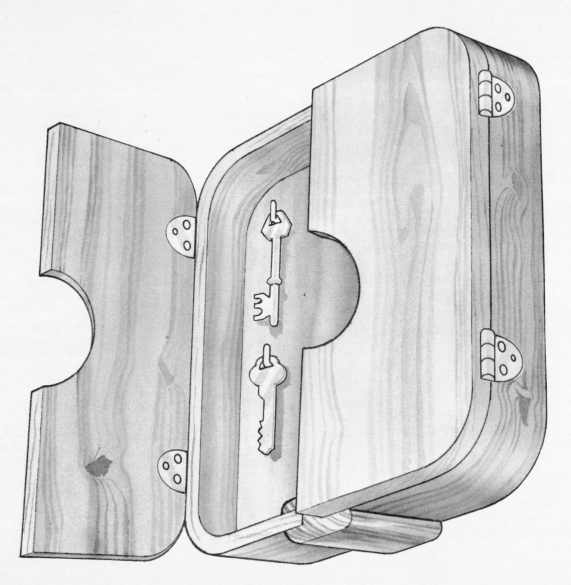

VENEERED KEY CUPBOARD

MATERIAL

veneer of birch, ash or beech,
    0.6–1.0 mm (about 1/32″) thick
solid wood for doors, back and splicing
    joints
adhesive (phenolic resin or
    polyurethane)

TOOLS

planer
bandsaw
circular saw
router
sash or screw cramps
veneer saw
putty knife
marking gauge

To make these instructions easy to
follow, we have given exact measurements, but feel free to adapt them to
your own needs.

1

Start by making a mould for the cupboard. Plane a 50×200 mm (2″×8″) board, 600 mm (24″) long, and draw one half of the cupboard on the wood: length 300 mm (12″), width 140 mm (5½″), corner radius 50 mm (2″).

Use the bandsaw to saw exactly along the line.

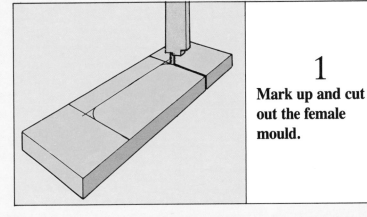

1
Mark up and cut out the female mould.

2

Decide on the thickness of the cupboard walls — let us say 10 mm (⅜″) — and mark the thickness with a marking gauge on the male part. Cut exactly along the line with the bandsaw. You now have a mould consisting of two parts, male and female, and the distance between them is the same as the intended thickness of the walls.

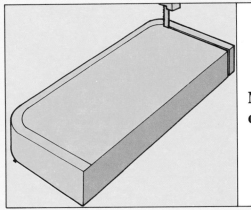

2
Mark up and cut out the male mould.

3

Cut 50 mm (2″) wide veneer strips, about 600 mm (24″) long, using the veneer saw. Put them together to achieve the intended thickness, and try them out in the mould using sash or screw cramps.

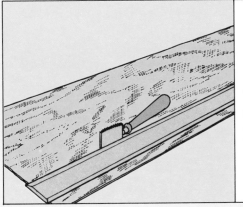

3
Cut out as many strips of veneer as you need.

4

Place paper between the mould and the veneer to avoid gluing the strips onto the mould. Spread the adhesive resin with a small putty knife on the top side of all the veneer strips except the last one. Lay the strips together, being careful to level them off. Then use the female part (*a*) to press them up against the male part (*b*), and tighten with cramps.

One half of the cupboard is now complete. Repeat the procedure for the other half.

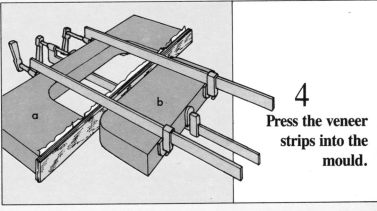

4
Press the veneer strips into the mould.

5
Plane the long edges and cut the short ends to size.

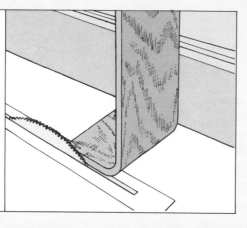

5
When the adhesive has hardened, carefully plane one of the long edges of each half. Then trim the opposite side in the circular saw with the aid of the rip fence.

Cut the short ends to their exact size.

6
Make a jointing strip and cut out a groove.

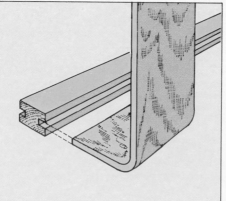

6
In order to join the two halves together, make a jointing strip 20×30×250 mm (¾"×1⅛"×10"). Cut a groove, 10×10 mm (⅜×⅜") with the saw or the router along the two opposite sides. Test the fit on one of the two side sections, and adjust as necessary.

7
Cut strips to make the doors and back.

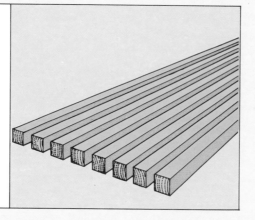

7
To make the doors and back, use a piece 650 mm (25½") long. Plane one side and one edge, then cut into lengths 20×20 mm (¾"×¾"). Plane all sides.

Make sure that all the lengths have vertical grain at the ends. Mark them so as not to mix them up when gluing.

8
Glue the strips together.

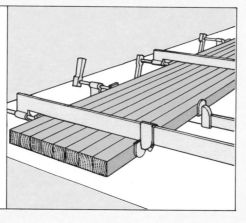

8
Assemble these pieces to form a pattern with heartwood against heartwood core and sapwood against sapwood. Ensure that the width is a few centimetres (about 1") wider than the finished cupboard. Glue together with wood adhesive and cramps.

9

When the glue has dried, plane the assembled piece and cut it in half to make the back and front pieces.

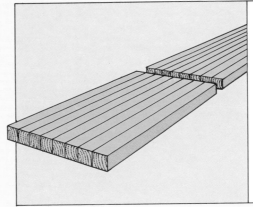

9

Plane one face and one edge. Saw in two.

10

Plane off a further 12 mm (½") from the back piece.

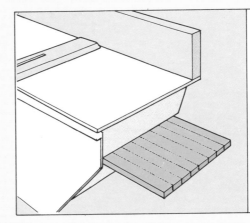

10

Plane the back piece more than the front.

11

Cut the jointing strip to form two joints with the depth of the side. Smooth and round off the edges of the joints, and smooth down the inner and outer surfaces of the sides. Glue together the sides and the joints with wood adhesive, using a piece of string or elastic strap cramps for tightening.

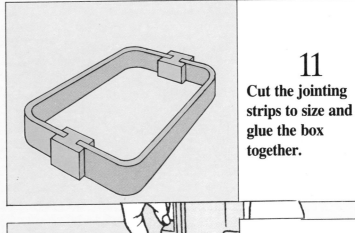

11

Cut the jointing strips to size and glue the box together.

12

Make a 12 mm (½") deep rebate round the back of the cupboard, using the router and a 7 mm (¼") cutter with a guide pin.

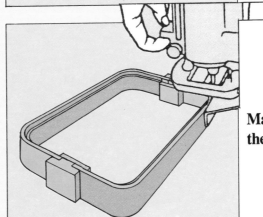

12

Make a rebate for the cupboard back.

13

Mark up and cut out the back piece. Pre-drill.

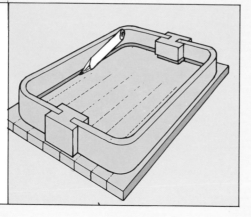

13

Place the cupboard on top of the back piece, and trace the shape of the cupboard. Cut with the bandsaw. Note that the back should be 2 mm (¹⁄₁₆″) narrower than the position of the rebate. Pre-drill all round with a 1.5 mm (¹⁄₁₆″) drill, and fix the back with small brads through the drilled holes.

14

Make two halves of the front piece. Mark up the door.

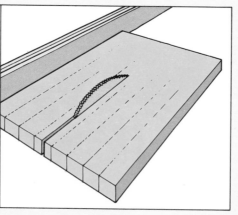

14

Cut the front piece in two. Plane an edge on each half, and place the planed edges adjacent to each other. Place the cupboard on top and trace the outline.

15

Cut out the doors. Smooth down.

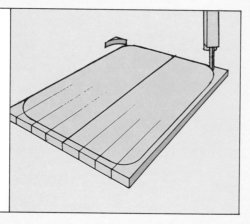

15

Cut out with the bandsaw. Smooth down the edges with abrasive paper and a sanding block.

16

Mark up the hinges and screw them in position.

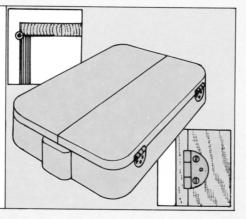

16

Mark the hinges on each of the doors and on the sides. (The centre of the hinges should be one sixth of the door's height from the top and bottom edges of the door — this is a rule of thumb for doors up to 1300 mm/51″.) The hinges are placed so that the centre of the pin is outside the line of the door; if they are placed deeper, the door cannot be completely opened, since its edge will catch the side of the cupboard.

Screw on the hinges, but do not use all the screws at first, so that it is easier to make any necessary adjustments.

17

When the doors have been adjusted to align with the cupboard's outer edges, knobs can be added for opening the doors. Plane the central edges so that the gap between the doors is 1.5 mm (1/16").

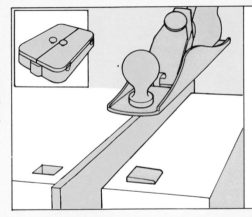

17

Plane between the doors. Attach knobs.

18

An alternative to door knobs is a hole between the doors, which can be made by drilling. To secure the doors, use two spring-catches of appropriate size. Screw key hooks to the back.

Finishing

Use oil or a thin coat of varnish. Smooth down with fine steel wool until smooth.

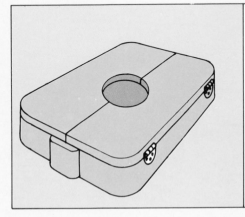

18

Alternative to door knobs. A neatly shaped hole.

CHESSBOARD

MATERIAL
oak and ash
plywood or chipboard
adhesive tape
ammonia

TOOLS
planer
circular saw
sash and screw cramps
slide gauge

Preparation
Cut a piece of plywood or chipboard to size, 385×385×12 mm (15¼"× 15¼"×½"). Make sure the corners are at right angles.

1
Cut lippings and glue two to opposite sides of the board.

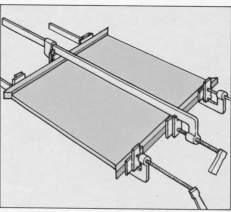

1
Cut and plane a piece of oak or ash to form lippings (side strips for gluing on), 10 mm×15 mm (⅜"×⁹⁄₁₆"). Cut mitres in the corners, and glue the lippings on two opposite edges of the board. Use sash cramps and lengths of wood for holding in place.

2
Plane the lippings level with the board.

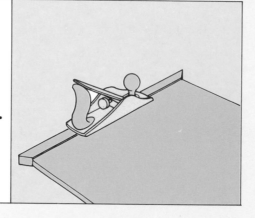

2
When the glue has dried, plane the glued-on lippings level with the board.

3
Glue on the other two lippings.

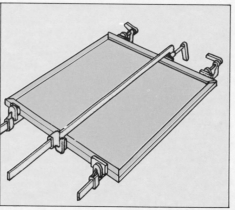

3
Glue on and plane the other two lippings in similar fashion.

4

Take a length of oak and one of ash for making the squares of the chessboard. Cut them into smaller pieces 55 mm (2³⁄₁₆″) wide, then plane one face and one edge to make them exactly 50 mm (2″) wide. The measurement must be exact, so check with a slide gauge. Then cut the pieces into laminae 3.5 mm (just over ⅛″) thick, using the circular saw.

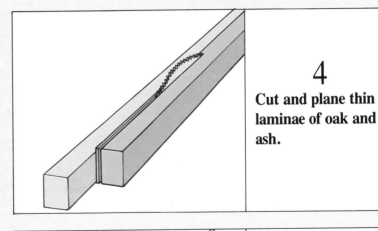

4

Cut and plane thin laminae of oak and ash.

5

Screw an auxiliary fence — a straight, planed piece of wood (*a*) — onto the mitre fence (*b*) of the circular saw in such a way that it is 20 mm (¾″) past the blade, and thus provides support from behind while cutting. Fasten a stop block (*c*) to the rip fence (*d*), then check the distance between the block and the blade with one of the 3.5 mm (⅛″) thick laminae to make sure the saw will cut 50 mm (2″) exactly.

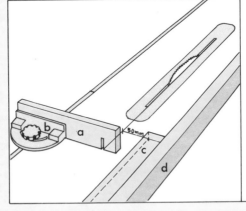

5

Set the circular saw to cut 50 mm (2″) pieces.

6

Check that the angle between the blade and the mitre fence is exactly 90° by taking a piece of scrap wood whose sides are parallel and cutting a narrow piece from the end; then turn it over and cut off another narrow piece.

Measure with a sliding gauge at both ends; if they are exactly the same, the angle is 90°. If not, adjust the mitre fence and check again, until the result is 90° and the piece is parallel.

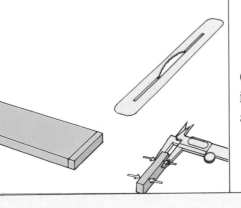

6

Check that the saw is cutting at right angles.

7

Before cutting the other lengths, cut some trial pieces and adjust until the samples are exactly square, measured with a slide gauge. When you are satisfied, the squares of the chessboard can be cut.

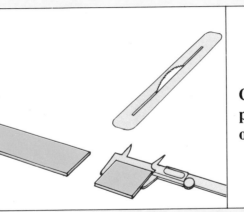

7

Cut some sample pieces before cutting out the squares.

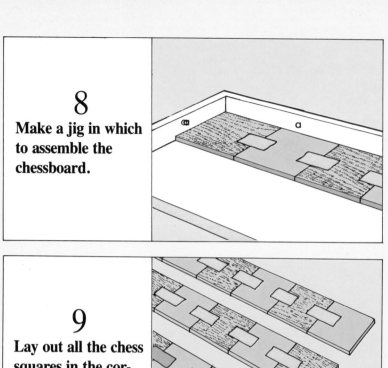

8

Make a jig in which to assemble the chessboard.

9

Lay out all the chess squares in the correct pattern.

10

Tape over the joins.

11

Cut and glue a support base for the pieces.

8

The easiest way of assembling the squares is to make a simple jig with a piece of chipboard 500 mm×150 mm (20″×6″). Strips (*a*), 10 mm×50 mm (⅜″×2″), are nailed onto two adjacent edges of the chipboard. Using the strip as a border, place the squares in position, alternately oak and ash, with the grain in the same direction. Secure with adhesive tape in the middle of each square and place eight in a row.

9

Each row should start with oak or ash alternately in the final arrangement.

10

To form the chessboard, stick the eight rows together with tape in the same way as you stuck the loose squares. Finish off by sticking a length of tape over each joint, to avoid glue penetration.

11

Cut strips (*a*) 400 mm (15¾″) long, of equal width and of the same material as the squares, to serve as a support base; glue together oak and ash alternately. The base prevents the finished board from warping. The finished construction will therefore have three layers, the squares, the plywood, and the support base.

Make sure the base is exactly square. Allow to dry.

12

When gluing the taped pieces and support base to the plywood, use two sheets (*a*) of 19 mm (¾″) chipboard, each about 25 mm (1″) wider than the finished chessboard. Place paper between the sheets and the faces of the board, and secure with eight screw cramps and tape.

The wood adhesive should be spread as quickly as possible. Place the squares and base in position, and fix with tape round all the corners to prevent shifting. Tighten gently with a cramp in each corner. First tighten across the diagonals, then tighten the other cramps in between.

When the adhesive has dried, use a cabinet scraper to remove the tape, then smooth down the surface with abrasive paper. If the squares or base support have shifted slightly, the edges must be adjusted using the circular saw.

Smooth down and round off the edges.

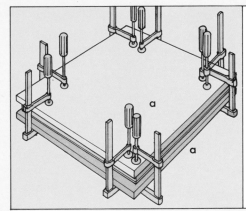

12

Glue the taped pieces and the support base to the plywood base.

13

In order to enhance the contrast between the two kinds of wood, the finished chessboard should be fumed by exposure to ammonia.

Find a cardboard box slightly larger than the chessboard, and four small blocks of wood about 45 mm×45 mm (1¾″×1¾″). Drill a hole for a match in each block so that the match sticks out about 25 mm (1″). Slot the matches into the holes, and place a small bowl or saucer and the four blocks inside the cardboard box.

Fill the saucer with concentrated ammonia, then place the chessboard on top of the matches and close the box QUICKLY. Seal the box with tape. Since ammonia is very volatile and evaporates rapidly, it is essential to act very quickly. Avoid inhaling the ammonia: if you must breathe, turn your head away.

Allow the box to stand for twenty-four hours before opening and checking. Add more ammonia and leave for another twenty-four hours if a darker colour is desired.

Smooth down if necessary with a fine abrasive paper.

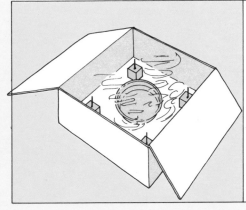

13

Give the finished board an ammonia bath.

Finishing
Polyurethane varnish.

DESK

MATERIAL
softwood or hardwood
plywood or hardboard for tongues

TOOLS
planer
circular saw
router
pillar drill
sash cramps
tenon saw
bevel gauge
marking gauge
scriber

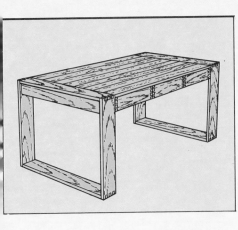

Component parts of the desk
(*a*) Table top made of boards
(*b*) Legs
(*c*) Floor rail
(*d*) Short rail
(*e*) Top cross rail
(*f*) Top support rail
(*g*) Drawer side
(*h*) Drawer front
(*i*) Drawer back
(*j*) Drawer bottom
(*k*) Drawer guides

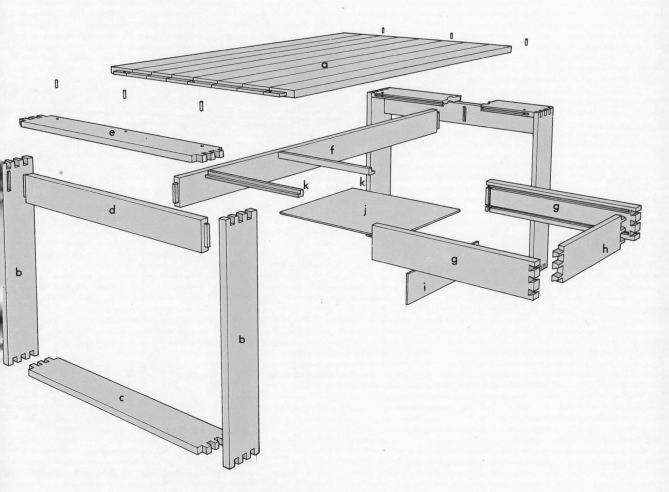

Preparation

Cut the boards for the table top. They should be no wider than 75 mm (3″), and preferably narrower.

Plane the face side and one of the edges of all the boards. Then plane the opposite edge of all the boards.

89

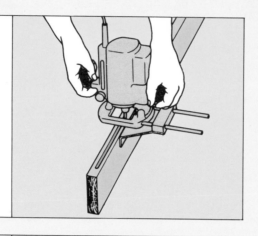

1
Rout out a groove for the tongues.

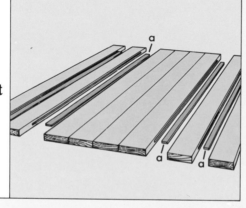

2
Cut tongues, lay out boards in pattern, and glue together.

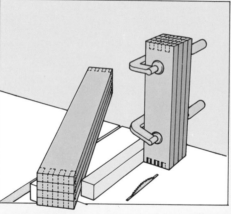

3
Make the legs and rails, box-joint them, and glue together.

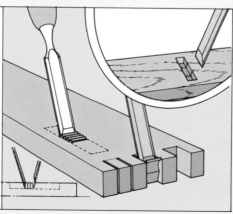

4
Mark and cut the mortises in the legs, short rails, and top cross rail.

1

Use the router to cut a groove for a tongue on all the board edges except for the two designated as outside edges. The grooves should be about 5 mm (³⁄₁₆″) wide and 5 mm (³⁄₁₆″) deep. If you do not have a router, you can use a circular saw.

2

Place the boards across trestles in such a way that the best surface pattern is obtained. Make sure all the boards are either heartwood or sapwood up. Number them in strict order, and draw a large triangle across the table top (this helps alignment when the top is being glued together).

Cut tongues (*a*) of plywood or hardboard 1 mm (¹⁄₁₆″) thinner than the combined width of two grooves: about 5 mm (³⁄₁₆″) + 5 mm (³⁄₁₆″) − 1 mm (¹⁄₁₆″) = about 9 mm (⁵⁄₁₆″).

Glue the top together using sash cramps (see pages 65–66).

Cut the table top to size, remembering to allow for the tenons.

3

Rough-cut the pieces for legs and rails. Plane all the pieces, then cut them to their correct lengths. Cramp the pieces together and cut box joints (see pages 57–59, which shows cutting box joints with a circular saw).

4

Mark mortises in the top parts of the legs, corresponding to the tenons of the short rails. Mark mortises in the middle of the short rails corresponding to the tenons of the top support rail. Finally, mark a long mortise in the top cross rails corresponding to the tenons of the table top.

Cut all these mortises. Use the pillar drill and chisel for cutting the holes in the legs and short rails, and the router for cutting the long mortises in the top cross rails.

The left-hand picture shows the cutting of a mortise in the leg, for the tenon in a short rail.

The inset picture shows a mortise in a short rail, for one of the tenons in the top support rail.

The cutting of the long mortises in the top cross rails is as in picture 2.

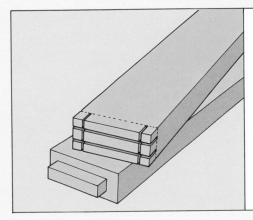

5
Make the tenons in the rails.

5

Make the tenons in the short rails and in the top support rail in the same way as those in the short stretchers of the coffee table (page 62).

The picture shows the saw cuts in the end of the top support rail and, below it, the finished tenon.

6

Join together (but do not glue) the two pairs of legs, so that you have two leg frames. Mark the tenons (a) on the table top. They should fit into the long mortises (b) of the top cross rails. Cut the tenons with the router.

Drill four 5 mm (³⁄₁₆″) holes for screws along the top support rail (c) for fixing the table top. Countersink with a 10 mm (⅜″) drill until 20 mm (¾″) remains (see the small picture at bottom right).

Bevel the top edge (d) of each end of the table top. Use the router with a suitable cutter positioned so that the bevel is about 1 mm (¹⁄₁₆″) (see the small inset picture at top middle).

Fit the top into the leg frames. Measure the distance between them, subtract 6 mm (¼″) and divide the resultant figure into three (which gives the lengths of the drawer fronts). Also measure the distance between the long side of the table top and the top support rail. This will be the depth of the drawers.

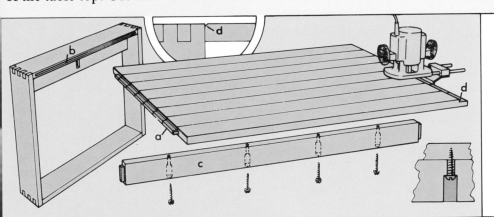

6
Rout out tenons on the table top. Fit the top into the leg frames. Drill holes in the top support rail. Measure the depth of the drawers.

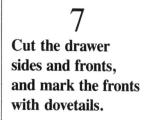

7

Cut the drawer sides and fronts, and mark the fronts with dovetails.

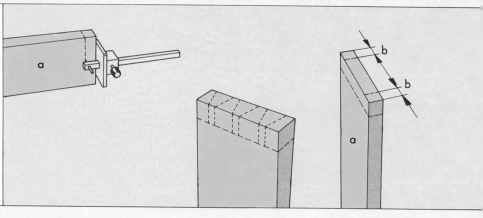

7

Cut six pieces to lengths equal to twice the drawer depth. These shall be the drawers' sides. Cut the pieces for the fronts and backs of the drawers. Allow an extra 6 mm (¼″) on all measurements. Plane all the pieces.

Cut the drawer sides and fronts to their correct lengths. (Wait until stage 13 before cutting the backs.) Set a marking gauge to the thickness of the drawer sides and mark it on the drawer fronts (*a*), as in the top picture.

Measure about 12 mm (½″) on each side of the ends of the drawer fronts (lines (*b*), marked in the picture at right).

Then divide the intermediate section into an odd number of parts. Mark out the sloping lines of the dovetails on the end-wood of the drawer fronts, using a bevel gauge set at about 10°. Continue the lines down to the marked lines, using a set square (see the centre of the picture).

8

Saw and chisel the sockets on the drawer fronts.

8

Cut the sockels with a tenon saw. Be careful to saw at right angles to the piece and at the waste side of the line. Cut out the waste material with a chisel (see step 11).

9

Use the sockets to mark tails on the drawer sides.

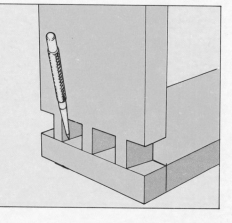

9

Measure the thickness of a drawer front and transfer it to the drawer side with a marking gauge. Stand the drawer front on the drawer side and mark the tails.

Mark the fronts and sides so that they don't get mixed up later on.

10

Cut out the tails with a tenon saw. Note that the scribed line should be bisected in order to ensure a good fit (i.e., half of the scribed line should remain after the cutting). To avoid cutting on the wrong side of the scribed line, mark all the pieces to be removed with a cross, then cut away the wood in between as in point 11. Test to see if the pins fit, and if not, trim carefully with a chisel. The pins must be a close fit.

11

Trim the tails with a chisel that is a fraction narrower than, or equal to, the width of the tail.

(*Top picture*) Start by cutting about 2 mm (¹⁄₁₆″) from the marked base line of the tail. Then cut in towards this first cut, but save the base line (and the outer edge) so as not to break the end when cutting from the opposite side.

(*Bottom picture*) Turn the piece over. The tail is now lying with its point down against the working surface. Cut in the same way as on the other side. When the piece has come loose, trim away the remaining 2 mm (¹⁄₁₆″) at the base of the tail with the chisel.

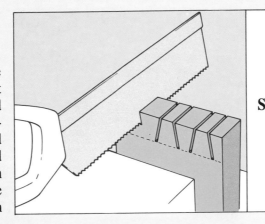

10
Saw the tails.

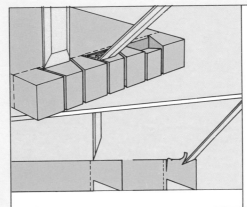

11
Clean out the waste with a chisel.

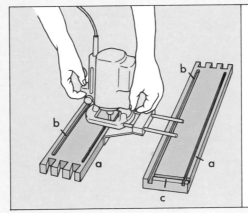

12
Rout out grooves in the drawer sides for the bottom and back.

12

Cut the drawer sides to their correct length. Make grooves (*a*) for the drawer bottom in the sides, but stop about 5 mm (³⁄₁₆″) short of the dovetailed ends. Cut the grooves (*b*) for the runners; they should be 10 mm (³⁄₈″) wide, about 5 mm (³⁄₁₆″) deep, and 10 mm (³⁄₈″) from the upper edge.

Use the same cutter to make a groove (*c*) for the back, between the two grooves (*a*) and (*b*) but about 20 mm (¾″) from the back edge, and also to make a groove for the drawer bottom in the front piece.

13

Cut the drawer back to size. Give it tenons and notches.

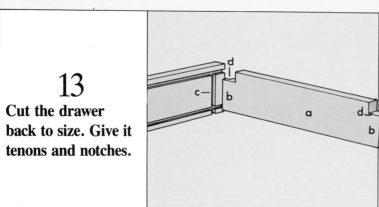

14

Glue the legs into frames.

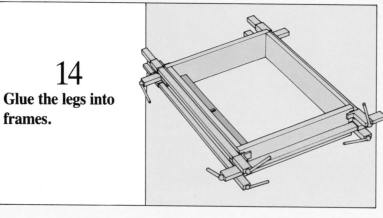

15

Glue the leg frames to the top support rail.

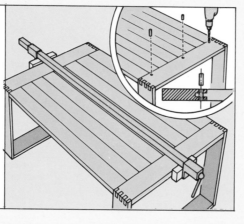

16

Assemble the drawers and glue together.

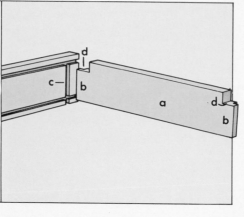

13

Establish the inside measurement of the drawer, which is equal to the front piece minus the pins, and add 10 mm (⅜″) to give the required length of the back piece. Cut the drawer back (*a*) to its correct size.

Then use the circular saw to cut tenons (*b*) to fit the grooves (*c*). Adjust the height of the back, which should be equal to the distance from the upper edge of the drawer to the top of the drawer's bottom groove. Cut out two notches (*d*), 23×23 mm (⅞″×⅞″), for the runners.

14

Now glue together the pairs of legs into frames, using sash cramps to press them together in both directions. Check the angles and allow the frames to dry before smoothing them.

15

Glue the leg frames to the top support rail. Note that the table top must be in position before the top support rail is glued. The table top should not be glued to the top cross rails, but should be movable in its groove. Fix the table top with three wooden plugs drilled through the top cross rail and the pins of the table top (see inset).

16

Before assembling the drawers, smooth the insides. Then glue the drawers together with the aid of sash cramps. Check that the diagonals of the drawers are equal to verify the right angles, and check that the drawers are flat by standing them on a flat surface.

17

Cut the drawer bottoms (*a*). Start by cutting the plywood to the required width, and notch the front corners since the grooves (*b*) only go as far as the dovetail. Push the bottom piece into the groove, mark the depth by drawing a line between the back edges of the drawer sides, and then cut the bottom piece. Sand the bottom before sliding it into place.

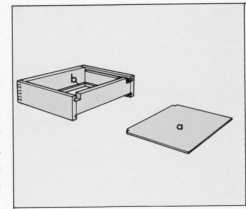

17
Cut the drawer bottoms and notch the front corners. Insert but don't nail yet!

18

Cut runners (*a*) 22×22 mm (⅞″×⅞″) and make a notch (*b*) in them, 13.5×6.5 mm (½″×¼″). Trim them to their correct size. Drill three 4 mm (⁵⁄₃₂″) holes in each runner and countersink the holes for the screw heads.

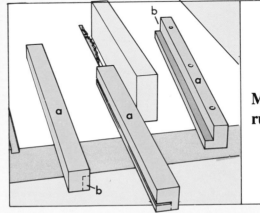

18
Make the drawer runners.

19

When fitting the runners, turn the table upside down. Remove the drawer bottoms and put the drawers into position before screwing on the runners. If the drawers do not run smoothly, try sanding the bottom edges of the runners. They can also be lubricated with paraffin wax, but in that case wait until they have been treated, or there may be stains where the varnish will not dry.

Replace the bottoms in the drawers and secure them with small pins through the back section.

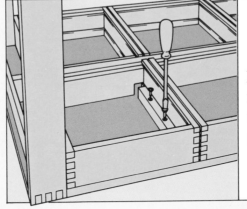

19
Fit the runners and nail the drawer bottoms in place with pins.

Finishing

Use a semi-matt polyurethane varnish, applied with brush or spray. In order to get a smooth surface, the first coat of varnish should be thinned with 20–30% thinner. When dry, smooth down with abrasive paper of no. 360 grit, or use a steel scraper for the large surfaces. Thin the second coat with 10% thinner. Apply the varnish liberally with long strokes and avoid overlapping more than necessary. Should the surface be patchy and uneven when the varnish is dry, smooth down with fine steel wool to give a matt surface. Always smooth down along the grain.

CHEST OF DRAWERS

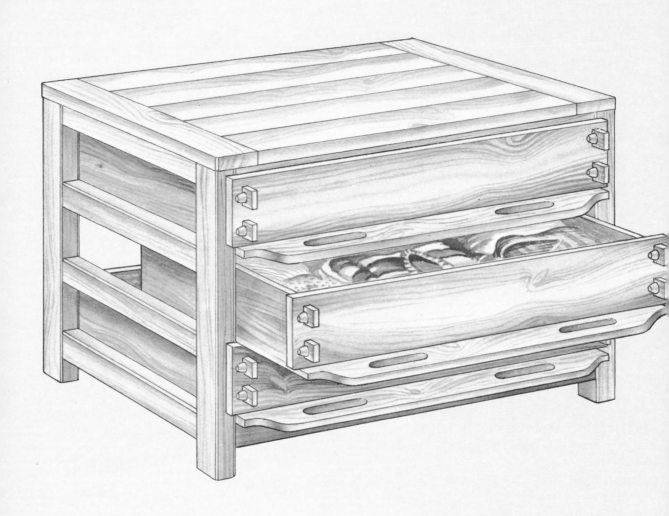

MATERIAL
hardwood or softwood
plywood

TOOLS
planer
circular saw
pillar drill
smoothing plane
knot borer
router

96

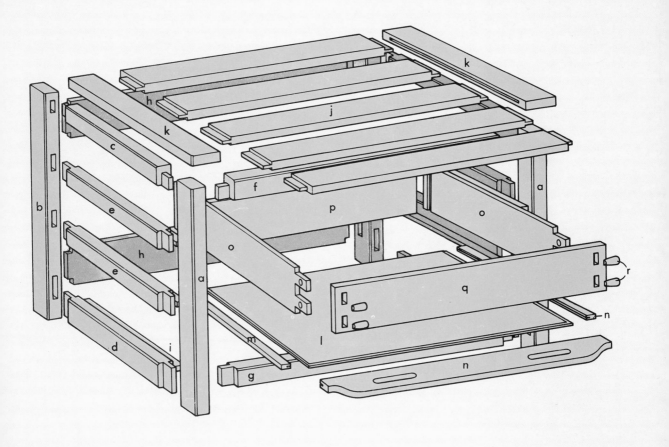

The parts of the chest of drawers

(a) Front posts
(b) Rear posts
(c) Upper side rail
(d) Lower side rail
(e) Drawer guide (there are two on each side)
(f) Upper front rail
(g) Lower front rail
(h) Upper and lower back rails
(i) Drawer runner
(j) Top of chest (glued strips)
(k) Cross member
(l) Drawer bottom
(m) Solid wood lipping (edging)
(n) Drawer handle
(o) Drawer side
(p) Drawer back
(q) Drawer front
(r) Dowel

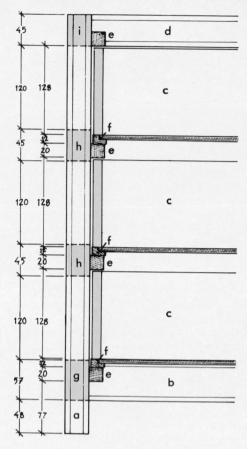

The complete construction drawings of this piece of furniture are to be found on pages 24–27.

(a) Post
(b) Lower front rail
(c) Drawer back
(d) Upper front rail
(e) Drawer runner
(f) Lipping
(g) Lower side rail
(h) Drawer guide
(i) Upper side rail

Preparation

Saw up strips, 900 mm (35″) and 1100 mm (43″), for the front and side rails and drawer guides, from a 1½″×6″ plank. Plane one face and one edge of each strip, and saw them again into strips that are approximately 48 mm (1⅞″) wide. One strip must be at least 25 mm (1″) wider than the others, as it is to be used for the lower side rails, which will also function as drawer guides for the bottom drawers. Plane

one edge of each strip, and then feed them through the planer so that their final dimensions are 45×35 mm (1¾″×1⅜″) for all the strips except the lower side rails, which are to be 57×35 mm (2¼″×1⅜″).

Now saw the posts, 600 mm (24″) long. Mark up mortises for the upper and lower side rails. Divide the intervening distance between these mortises so that you will get exactly the same distance between the drawer guides. This sounds pretty complicated, but see the drawing on the left, which shows how this functions on one example. Mark up these mortises on the posts. The mortises are to be exactly the same height as the upper side rail and the drawer guides, that is, 45 mm (1¾″). The mortise for the lower side rail will be 57 mm (2¼″). Note! The tenons for the upper side rails and the upper front rail are not the full width of the rails, but are reduced from the top by 15 mm (⅝″), becoming therefore 30 mm (1¼″) high.

Another finesse is that the lower front rail is placed so that its bottom aligns with the bottom of the lower side rail. This means that the lower side rails are 12 mm (½″) higher up than the lower front rail, thus holding the bottom drawer in place.

Mark up also mortises for the rear rails, 95 mm long and placed 50 mm (2″) in from the top and bottom of the rear posts.

Make sure that the mortises for the side rails are marked out exactly in the middle of the posts. Mortises for the front and rear rails must be positioned so that they align with the outer edges of the posts.

Cut out the mortises with the pillar drill and chisel (see page 62).

Measure the depth of the mortises and mark up the dimensions of the tenons on the rails and drawer guides. Cut the rails and guides to the right length and cut out the tenons on the circular saw (see page 47).

1

Sand down all surfaces of the prepared pieces and bevel all edges with the smoothing plane. Glue side rails, drawer guides, and posts together with the aid of sash cramps so that you have two sets of side frames. Measure the diagonals to check that the side frames are in square and check that they are in true by holding them up and sighting them—if they are in true, the front post will cover the rear post in your line of vision. If not, correct by adjusting the sash cramps.

2

When the side frames have dried, glue them to the front and rear rails to form the carcase. Check once again the diagonals. Everything must be square and in true.

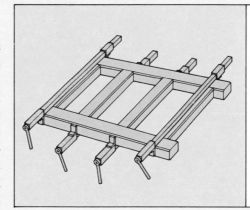

1

Glue the side frames together.

2

Glue the carcase together.

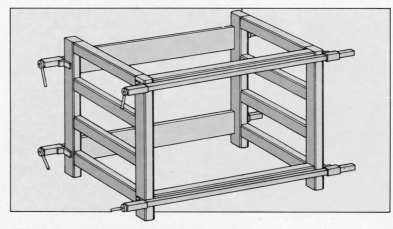

3

Cut up the drawer runners. Drill screw holes.

4

Screw the runners into position, on the upper and lower side rails. The runner (*a*) on the lower side rail (*b*) aligns with the top of the lower front rail (*c*). The runner on the upper side rail aligns with the bottom of the upper front rail.

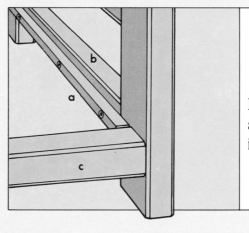

4

Fasten the upper and lower runners in place.

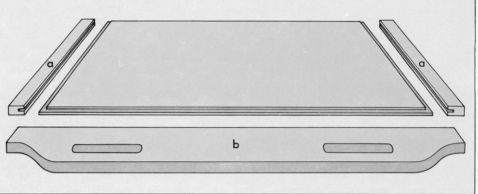

5
Saw the plywood bottoms and the lippings.

5

Make drawer bottoms from 6 mm (¼″) plywood. Fit each with a solid-wood 12×20 mm (½″×¾″) lipping (a) on the short sides. The front is fitted with a larger lipping (b), 12×65 mm (½″×2½″), which will double as the handle.

Make the lipping on the circular saw. Cut a groove in the lipping for the drawer bottom, about 3 mm (⅛″) from its edge and about 6 mm (¼″) deep.

Measure the distance between the insides of the front posts, take away the width of the lippings, and add 13 mm (½″) for the tenons. This gives you the width of the plywood for the drawer bottoms. The plywood depth is equal to the carcase depth minus the thickness of the back rail, plus 6 mm (¼″) for the tenons.

Saw the plywood. Saw a mortise on the sides and front that fits the groove in the lipping. They should be a tight fit. Cut the lippings to the right length.

6
Glue the side lippings on. Plane away any excess.

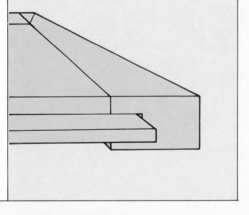

6

Glue the side lippings into position so that they are even with the shoulder of the tenon on the drawer bottom's front edge. When the glue has dried, plane it with the smoothing plane, so that the lipping lies flush with the plywood bottom. Before you glue the front lipping/handle into position, check that the drawer bottoms fit into the frame. If necessary, adjust by planing lightly. Mark the underneath of each drawer bottom with a number so that they don't get mixed up later.

7
Cut out the handle/lipping and glue in place.

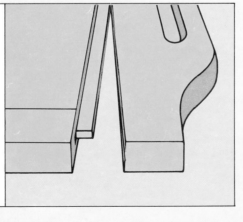

7

Cut the front lipping/handle to size (the same length as the drawer bottoms, which include the lippings). Mark up where the hand grips will be. Drill the first hole with a knot drill and saw out the rest of the waste with a fretsaw or a jigsaw.

Use the router to make a groove in

the lipping/handle for the tenon on the drawer bottom. Stop the groove before you get to the end of the lipping.

Glue the lipping/handles into place, so that they are level with the upper edge of the drawer bottom. When dry, adjust with the smoothing plane, if necessary.

8

The drawer backs and sides are sawn from 20×150 mm (¾"×6") planks. Cut six drawer sides and three backs. Ripsaw them in two, mark the pieces that were adjacent, and plane the face and the sawn edge. Glue them together with sash cramps. When dry, plane one face and one edge in the planer, to a thickness of 15 mm.

Cut the drawer sides and backs to their right heights (140 mm minus 12 mm for the lipping, or 5½" minus ½").

9

Put the lower drawer bottom in place and insert the drawer sides. With the top of the drawer sides as a guide, mark up where the drawer runners should be (leave some space between the top of the drawer and the runner). Screw the runners into place. Repeat for the next drawer. Mark the drawer sides with a triangle, the point of which points to the front, and number them 1, 2, and 3 from the top.

10

Saw the drawer fronts from a 25×200 mm (1"×8") plank which you rip-cut in two. Plane one face and one edge. Glue them together, using sash cramps. When dry, plane them down to 15 mm (⅝").

The drawer fronts must be 20 mm (¾") higher than the sides, to cover the runners. Mark these, too, with triangles, points outwards.

The drawer fronts should have the heartwood facing. Cut them to size,

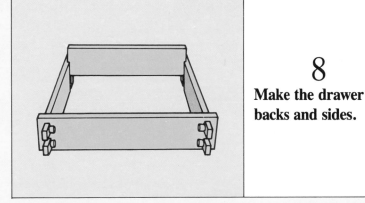

8
Make the drawer backs and sides.

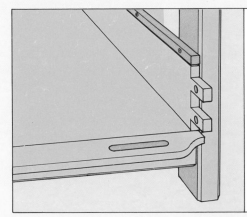

9
Position the other drawer runners and fasten in place.

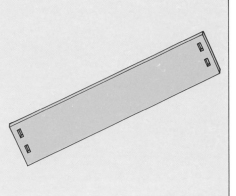

10
Make the drawer fronts and mortise them for the sides.

with 20 mm (¾") over on both sides.

Mark up the mortises on the fronts for the drawer sides' tenons. There should be a play of 3 mm (⅛") on either side to allow the drawer sides to run freely past the side frames.

Drill and chisel the mortises (see page 62). Make the tenons on the circular saw (see page 47).

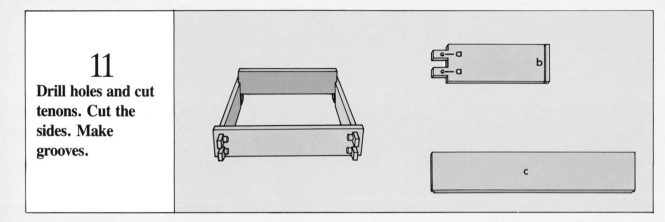

11

Drill holes and cut tenons. Cut the sides. Make grooves.

Drill a 15 mm (⅝″) hole (*a*) in the cheek of each tenon, with its centre 20 mm (¾″) from the shoulder.

Cut the drawer sides to length. They should be 360 mm (14″) long, measured from the shoulder of the tenon.

Saw a groove (*b*) on the circular saw to take the drawer back. It should be 20 mm (¾″) from the rear edge, 5 mm (³⁄₁₆″) wide and 5 mm (³⁄₁₆″) deep.

Cut the drawer back (*c*) to size and cut the tenons out on the circular saw. Smooth all the pieces.

12

Fasten drawer fronts with dowels. Fasten bottoms.

Make a piece of dowelling 15 mm (⅝″) in diameter from a rough peg that is hammered through a hole of the required diameter in a metal plate, as in the illustration on the left. Cut locking dowels, 50 mm (2″) long, and plane them on one side to a conical shape, so that they fit tightly in the drilled holes.

Put the drawer front in position,

lock it with the dowels, and glue the tenon on the drawer back. Now, fit and glue the drawer frame together.

When the drawer frame is dry, nail the bottom into place, with 30 mm (1⅛″) nails at 100 mm (4″) intervals. Countersink the nails.

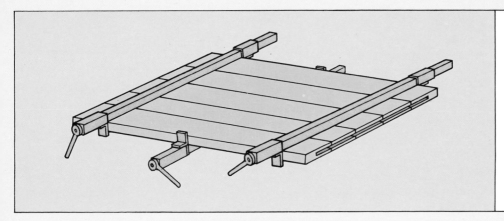

13

Make the top for the chest of drawers.

The top of the chest of drawers is built from a 25×200 mm (1″×8″) plank. Cross-cut it in 800 mm (32″) long pieces and rip-saw each into three equally wide strips. Plane one face and one edge. Glue together the three strips with sash cramps, with the heartwood side facing upwards. When dry, plane the faces and edges.

only glue two of the three rip-sawn pieces together (discard the third). The top of the chest needs to have only five strips to make up the proper depth.

Glue the two-strip and the three-strip sections together with the help of sash cramps. Smooth the surface with the smoothing plane.

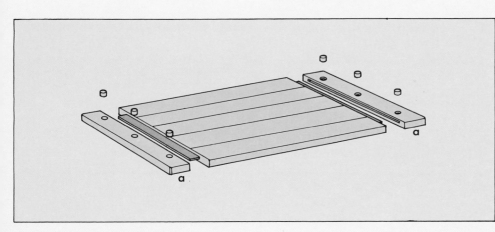

14

Make cross-members and fit. Screw top and carcase together.

Make two cross-members (a), 60×400 mm (2⅜″×16″), to edge the chest top. Make grooves, 8 mm (⁵⁄₁₆″) wide and 40 mm (1½″) deep. Finish them about 25 mm (1″) from the ends.

Cut the chest top to length—760 mm (30″), that is, 680 mm (27″) plus 80 mm (3″) for the tenons. Saw the tenons on the circular saw. Make the tenons 2 mm (⅛″) shorter than the mortises.

Smooth all the surfaces and bevel the edges. Fit together the cross-members and the top of the chest, using sash cramps but no adhesive. Drill three 10 mm (⅜″) holes through each cross-member and the tenons on the chest top. Lock them together with 10 mm (⅜″) glued dowels.

Screw the chest top to the carcase through holes in the upper rails.

Finishing
Varnish or oil.

BOOKCASE

MATERIAL
birch plywood, 19 mm (¾″),
  or solid birch
birch plywood, 6 mm (¼″)
hardboard
wire shelf holders

TOOLS
planer
circular saw
coping saw or bandsaw
router
pillar drill
sash cramps

It is essential to use material with good load-bearing qualities for the shelves. Our choice is either thick plywood, or strips of solid birch glued together. If the plywood is bought in sheets, their dimensions should allow them to be cut into three lengths of the same width as a shelf.

1

Start by cutting 330 mm (13″) wide lengths with the circular saw, then plane the edges. These will form the shelves and framework.

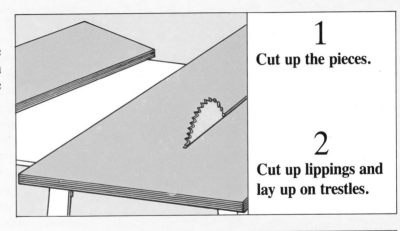

1

Cut up the pieces.

2

Cut up lippings and lay up on trestles.

2

Plane one edge of a 2050 mm (81″) long birch board, and cut 15 mm (⅝″) thick lippings for gluing onto all the long edges. Plane the lippings down to 13 mm (½″), then plane their width to 21 mm (¹³⁄₁₆″).

3

The easiest way to glue the lippings on is to place the lengths on trestles, with two lipping strips in between and one on each outer side, while outermost you place a protective batten.

Fix sash cramps in place, alternately above and below the material being glued together. Be careful to place the lippings centrally, so that they protrude both above and below.

4

When the glue has dried, plane away the excess wood from the lipping. Do this by securing the workpiece between the bench-stops; adjust the plane to a fine cut, and slant the blade from 0 to about 0.25 mm (less than ¹⁄₁₆″) from right to left. Plane at a slight angle to the direction of planing, so that most of the plane sole rests on the surface. If the wood is knotty, adjust the plane to a finer cut and check that the cap iron is set to about 1 mm (¹⁄₁₆″) from the edge of the blade.

Now the pieces for the sides, top, bottom, and shelves of the bookcase are ready. The next step is to fit the bookcase together.

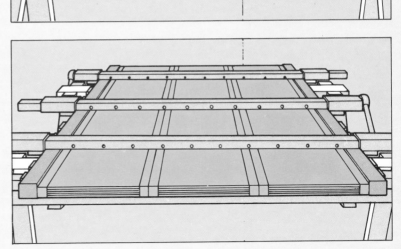

3

Glue lippings to the pieces.

4

Plane away excess wood from lippings.

5

Cut bookcase sides and top to size. Mitre where they will meet.

5

Start by cutting the sides and the top to length. Cut a mitre (*a*) at one end of the side piece, and mitres at both ends of the top. Set the blade at 45° for the mitre and cut with the aid of the mitre fence. Before cutting the mitre, check the angle by making trial cuts in discarded pieces of wood and ensure that the angle is right.

6

Rout tongue grooves in the mitres.

6

Make a 5 mm (³⁄₁₆″) groove for a tongue, about 7 mm (¼″) deep and 5 mm (³⁄₁₆″) from the base of the mitre. Use the router with the parallel guide. It helps to fix a board (*a*) as a support underneath the piece being worked on, level with the point of the mitre. It should be mitred in the other direction to prevent the point from sliding under the guide. End the groove about 15 mm (⅝″) from the front edge.

7

Make suitable tongues for the grooves.

7

Cut a plywood tongue (*a*), 13 mm (⁹⁄₁₆″) wide. Adjust the thickness so that it fits tightly into the groove.

8

Make rebates for the back and plinth in the sides.

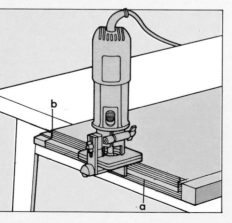

8

Make a rebate (*a*), 15 mm×19 mm (⅝″×¾″) in the sides at the bottom, but stop about 15 mm (⅝″) from the front edge. Adjust the router and make a rebate (*b*), 6 mm×10 mm (¼″×⅜″) for the back.

9

Make holes in the sides for wire shelf supports 250 mm (10″) long. Make a hardwood template for this purpose.

Cut a piece of hardboard the same length as the inside of the side piece. Start by marking a line 330 mm (13″) up from the bottom of the side piece, then mark at approximately 50 mm (2″) intervals in both directions, stopping about 100 mm (4″) from the bottom and the top respectively. The holes should be located in such a way that the shelf support is in the centre of the side section. Use a 3 mm (⅛″) bit. Mark the template with an arrow so that it is always the same way up, and secure it to the side with a cramp.

10

Fit the bit into the drill. Measure the total length of the bit and make a small depth-stop, which leaves only 15 mm (⅝″) of the bit exposed. Drill through this depth-stop and leave it on the bit, so that when you drill with the aid of the template, all holes will be of equal depth. Smooth down the inside of the bookcase frame before gluing together.

11

Cut the bottom 8 mm (⁵⁄₁₆″) shorter than the top. Then place one of the sides on the bottom and mark a rebate (*a*) in one front corner of the bottom. Repeat the procedure on the other side of the bottom section for the other side piece. Make the rebate using the circular saw with both the mitre and rip fences. Mark four screw holes at each end of the bottom section, starting about 30 mm (1¼″) from the front and back edges, and placing the other two holes at equal distances in between. The distance from the screwhole's centre to the edge should be 7 mm (just over ¼″).

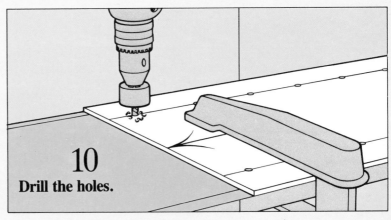

9

Make a template for the holes for the wire shelf holders.

10

Drill the holes.

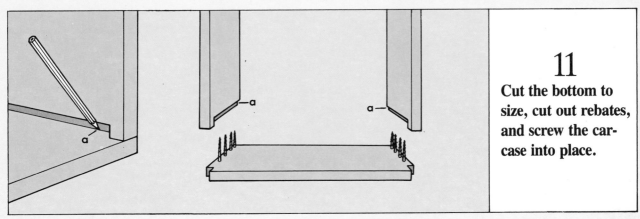

11

Cut the bottom to size, cut out rebates, and screw the carcase into place.

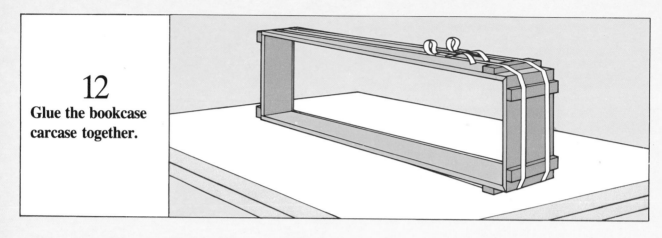

12
Glue the bookcase carcase together.

12

Start by gluing and screwing on the bottom, using a couple of sash cramps to hold the parts together. When gluing the mitred top corners, use a pair of strap cramps and four blocks of wood 350 mm (13¾″) long. Fasten the straps over the blocks, and tighten by moving the wood out towards the mitred corners.

Make the back of the bookcase from 6 mm (¼″) birch plywood. If you intend to spray varnish on the bookcase, do not nail down the back yet; otherwise fasten down with 25 mm (1″) panel pins at approximately 100 mm (4″) intervals.

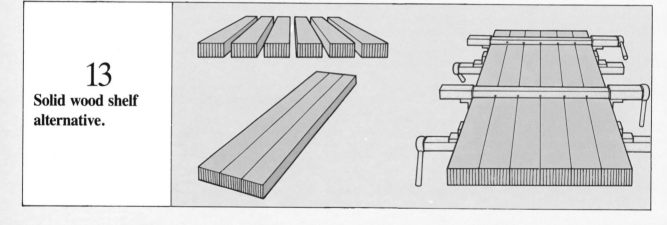

13
Solid wood shelf alternative.

13

If you have opted for making the shelves from strips of solid wood glued together lengthwise, the strips must not be wider than 30 mm (1¼″) and the grain should be vertical on the shelves.

Plane these sections as appropriate for the width of the plane. Having glued a number of sections together, plane and glue to the correct width, making sure that the joints are even.

Use a couple of screw cramps to hold sections together while securing the sash cramps above and below alternately.

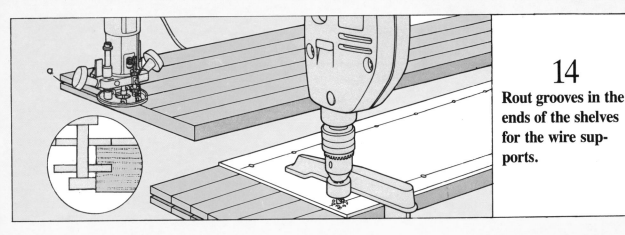

14

Rout grooves in the ends of the shelves for the wire supports.

14

The finished shelves must also have holes for shelf supports. The template used earlier is suitable for this purpose. Use it to mark the position of the holes on the shelf, being careful to centre them, and drill straight through with a 3 mm (⅛″) bit. To prevent the wood from splintering at the back, place a piece of chipboard underneath and use as high a speed as possible.

Make a groove (a) in both ends of the shelf for the wire shelf support, using the circular saw or the router and a 3 mm (⅛″) cutter. The depth of the groove should be 12 mm (½″) and stop 15 mm (⅝″) from the front edge.

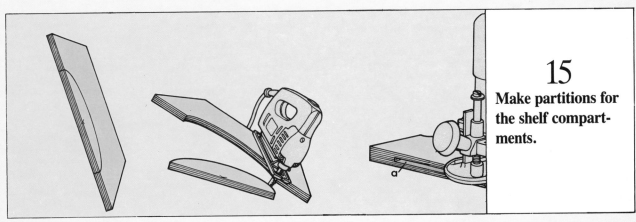

15

Use 6 mm (¼″) plywood to make partitions for record compartments of the same depth as the shelves. A decoration which also has a practical purpose is to form semicircular cut-outs in the partitions, with a radius of 100 mm (4″), thus making it easier to take out the records. The cut-outs are best formed with a coping saw or a band saw.

The partitions are supplied with a groove (a) for shelf supports in the top and bottom edges. These should stop 15 mm (⅝″) from the front edge, as in the shelves. Smooth down the edges of the partitions with abrasive paper glued to the edge of a piece of chipboard. Since it is difficult to glue lipping onto the thin plywood edge, these edges can be painted a suitable colour. Paint before the surfaces are smoothed.

16

Make the bookcase plinth. Mitre and glue the parts together.

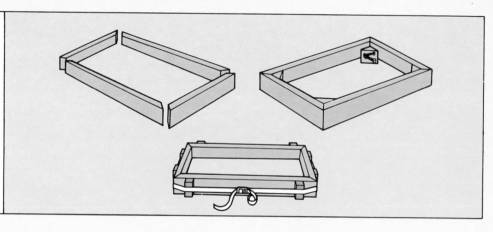

16

Either solid wood or plywood can be used to make the plinth, or kickboard, which should measure 10 mm (⅜″) less than the outer width of the bookcase and 30 mm (1¼″) less than its depth. Mitring is the easiest way of fastening the sections together (see page 45, but no reinforcing tongue is needed). Use a strap to hold the parts in place when gluing. When the glue has dried, strengthen the corners with pieces of wood screwed in position from the inside in both directions.

17

Screw the plinth to the bookcase.

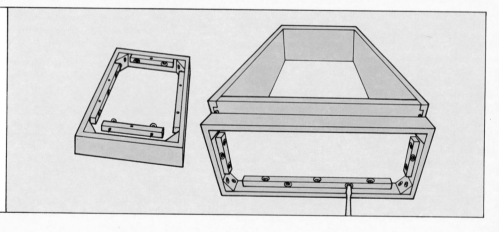

17

Cut two strips of wood 20 mm × 20 mm (¾″ × ¾″), equal to the inside measurement of the plinth between the corner pieces, and drill holes in two directions. Screw them onto the upper edge of the inside of the plinth, ready for fastening to the bookcase.

Finishing
Varnish or paint in a suitable colour.

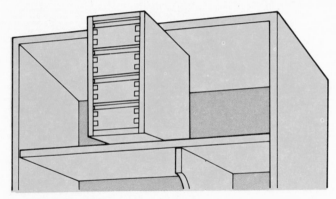

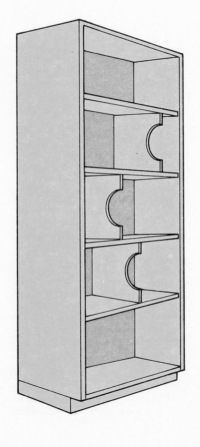

CASSETTE CABINET

Cassette storage is quite a problem for many people, and one solution is to build a made-to-measure cassette cabinet. The bookshelf that we have described on the previous pages can be fitted with the cassette cabinet that we now describe. Exact measurements that correspond with the measurements for the bookshelf are given below, so remember that if you change the dimensions for the bookshelf, you must make similar changes for the cassette cabinet.

However, there is nothing to stop you adapting this basic idea to suit your own needs. For instance, you might want to make a free-standing cassette cabinet, with its own pedestal (kickboard), or you might want to fit the cabinet into a stereo unit that you already have.

To make the cabinet as we describe it, you must first build the cabinet carcase (steps 1–5). Do not glue it together until you have made the four drawers (steps 6–16) and checked that they can be inserted easily into the carcase. Only then should the carcase be glued together.

1
Cut out the pieces for the carcase.

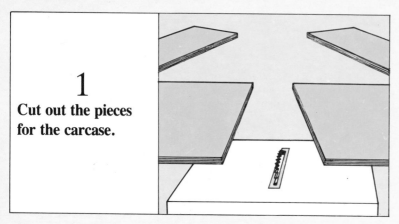

1

The cabinet carcase is made of 15 mm (5⁄8″) birch plywood. Cut the sheet to produce a length 320 mm (12⅝″) wide. From this, make two pieces 317 mm (12½″) long for the sides, and two pieces 155 mm (6¼″) long for the top and bottom.

2
Make grooves in the carcase sides.

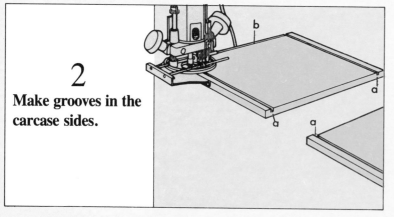

2

Make a 5 mm (3⁄16″) deep and 6 mm (¼″) wide groove (a) 15 mm (5⁄8″) from the top and bottom edges of the side pieces.

Make a groove (b) for the back 6×12 mm (¼″×½″) in the sides and in the pieces for the top and bottom, but note that the groove must stop 15 mm (5⁄8″) from the ends of the side pieces. Smooth down the inner surfaces.

3
Cut tenons in the carcase top and bottom.

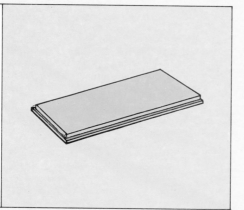

3

Use the circular saw to cut tenons in the top and bottom pieces. The tenons should fit tightly into the grooves and should be 0.5 mm (1⁄32″) shorter than the groove depth.

4
Make lippings and glue them to the fronts of the carcase pieces.

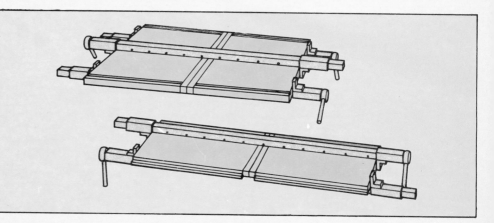

4

Glue a lipping on to all the front edges. The lippings should be 10×18 mm (⅜″×¾″) and are most easily glued by cramping the pieces adjacent to each other with the lippings in between. The picture shows pieces for the sides (*above*) and those for top and bottom (*below*) cramped together.

When the glue has dried, plane the lippings level with a smoothing plane, and trim the ends level. The lippings on the top and bottom pieces should be trimmed level with the shoulders of the tongues, so that they can fit into the grooves in the sides.

5

Cut the back from 6 mm (¼″) plywood, making sure it is square before assembling.

When all the parts of the cabinet itself are ready, it is time for the drawers to be made.

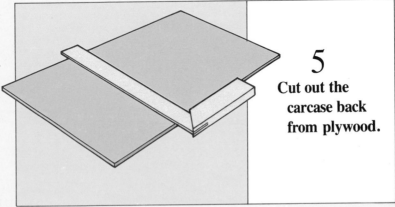

5

Cut out the carcase back from plywood.

6

Plane the wood for the sides and backs of the four drawers, 14×70 mm (⁹⁄₁₆″×2¾″). You are going to need four pieces about 800 mm (31½″) long.

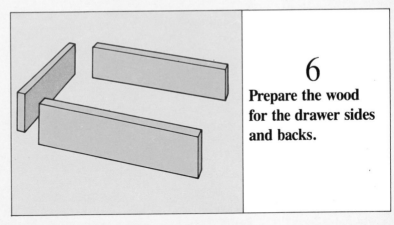

6

Prepare the wood for the drawer sides and backs.

7

Glue together and plane two pieces for each drawer front, which should be 20×95×145 mm (¾″×3¾″×5¾″). Make a groove with the router about 10 mm (⅜″) below the top edge of the front, so that a finger can be fitted in to facilitate opening.

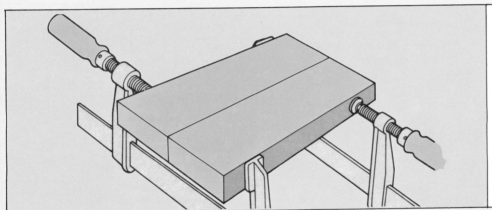

7

Prepare the drawer fronts and make a finger grip in each.

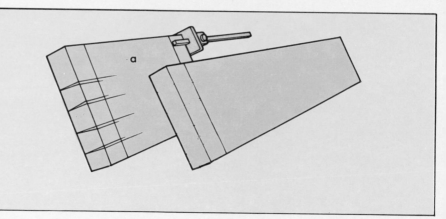

8

Mark up and cut out the drawer fronts and sides to size. Mark up the dovetail sockets on the drawer fronts.

8

Cut the fronts to 143 mm (5⅝"), and the sides to 310 mm (12¼").

Mark sockets on the fronts (*a*), using a marking gauge and bevel. Set to the thickness of the drawer sides and mark this all around the ends of the fronts.

The drawer fronts will be higher than the sides, so that you can get a grip on the cassettes from the side, when you want to put in or take out some cassettes. To mark up the dovetail sockets on the drawer fronts, mark a line on the end-wood 26 mm (1") from the top of the drawer. Mark a second line on the end-wood 12 mm (½") from the bottom of the drawer. Divide the intermediate space into three, and mark these dividing lines on the end-wood.

Set the bevel gauge to 10° and mark the sockets on the end-wood of the front drawers. Use a set square to continue the lines down to the socket shoulder (the first marked line).

In order to avoid cutting on the wrong side of the lines, mark the sockets with a cross.

9

Saw down and clean out the sockets.

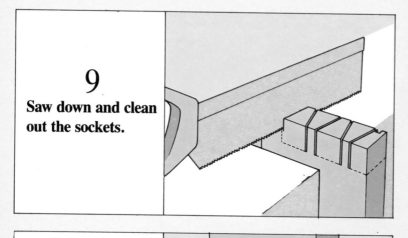

9

Cut with the tenon saw down to the shoulders of the sockets. Clean out the waste material with a chisel (see page 93).

10

Mark up the tails on the drawer sides.

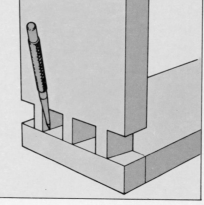

10

Use a marking gauge to transfer the thickness of the drawer fronts to the front ends of the drawer sides.

Place each drawer front against its corresponding side and mark the tails. Using a set square, square the lines over the end-wood of each side.

Mark the sides of each drawer with a triangle and a figure, with the point of the triangle pointing towards the front.

11

Bisect the marked lines with a tenon saw. It is important to saw exactly along the lines to produce a good fit.

Trim off the waste with a chisel, as on page 93.

Make sure the tails fit: if not, adjust with a sharp chisel.

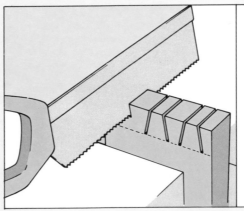

11

Saw down and clean out the tails.

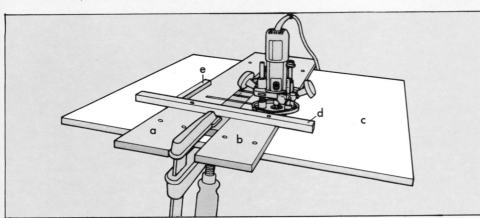

12

Mark up and rout out grooves in the drawer sides, using a special jig.

12

Mark at approximately 40 mm (1½″) intervals on the insides of the drawer for the movable partitions. Mark also grooves for the back and for the bottom.

A jig must be used so that the router will cut the grooves for the partitions, which do not run across the whole length of the piece, but stop at the groove cut for the bottom. Cut a couple of pieces (*a* and *b*) of 16 mm (¹¹⁄₁₆″) chipboard or 15 mm (⅝″) plywood, about 600 mm (23⅝″) long and 150 mm (6″) wide.

Fix them to a sheet of chipboard (*c*) at a distance from each other equal to the height of the drawer side. Then nail on a batten (*d*) at right angles to the chipboard pieces (*a* and *b*) about 200 mm (8″) from one edge.

Screw a block (*e*) on to the chipboard (*a*) as a stopper, so that the router does not overshoot the groove for the bottom piece.

Then adjust the depth of the router to about 5 mm (³⁄₁₆″). Choose a 6 mm (¼″) cutter and cut along the batten (*d*), using the router sole as a guide against batten. This groove will serve as a guide when the other grooves are made in the drawer sides.

Place the drawer side between the chipboard pieces with its inside uppermost, secure with a cramp, and make the grooves for the partitions and the back, one at a time. For each new groove, move the drawer side the appropriate amount along the jig.

13

Cut bottoms, partitions, and backs to size. Make grooves in the sides and fronts. Make tongues in the backs.

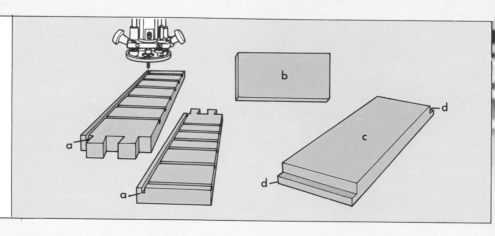

13

Cut grooves (*a*) in the sides and fronts for the drawer bottoms, which you cut out from 6 mm (¼″) plywood or hardwood. Cut out the partitions (*b*) from the same material. The grooves should be 5 mm (³⁄₁₆″) deep, and they should end 10 mm (³⁄₈″) from the front edges.

Cut the backs (*c*) to size. They should have the inside measurements of the drawer plus 10 mm (³⁄₈″) on the length to allow for the tongues (*d*), which you now cut out with a circular saw.

14

Assemble and glue together the drawer pieces.

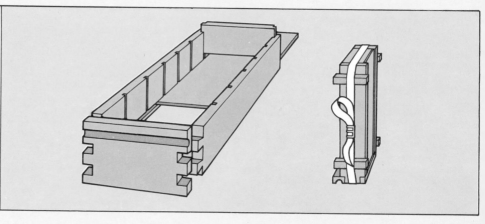

14

Smooth down the inner sides and the bottom of the drawer. Glue together the front, back and sides. Slide the bottom in and fasten it with panel pins to the back only. The picture on the right shows one of the four drawers being held together by a strap cramp while the glue is setting.

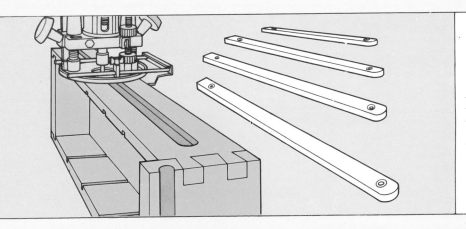

15

Make a 20 mm (¾″) groove in the middle of each side. (The drawers are supposed to slide on runners which fit these grooves.) Stop 25 mm (1″) before the router reaches the front edge.

Cut and plane runners for the grooves, round off one end and cut to length.

16

Assemble the cabinet carcase without gluing the parts together. Secure it with sash cramps.

Insert the bottom drawer. Allow a tiny space between it and the bottom of the carcase, and mark the position of its runners from the back of the carcase.

Repeat the procedure with the other drawers.

Pre-drill the runners and countersink for two screws, then fasten them to the cabinet sides as marked. Adjust the positions and/or thickness, so that the drawers slide easily in and out.

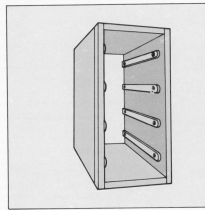

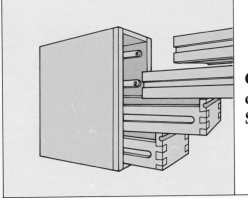

17

Glue the cabinet carcase together and assemble the back. Smooth down and round off all edges.

When the glue has dried, try inserting the drawers. If they do not slide in and out easily, paraffin wax applied to the runners may help.

Finishing

Use a polyurethane-based varnish with UV (ultraviolet) protection in order to prevent the birch from yellowing.

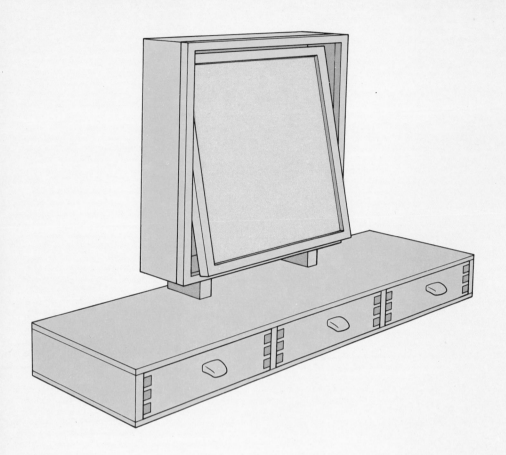

VANITY MIRROR

MATERIAL
pine
plywood, 6 mm (¼″) thick
birch pole, 10 mm (⅜″) diameter
brass bar, 5 mm (³⁄₁₆″) diameter
spiral spring
mirror glass

TOOLS
circular saw
planer
router
tenon saw

Preparation
Begin with the "chest" of drawers. For
the carcase, cut six 1200 mm (48″)
lengths of pinewood, 25×150 mm
(1″×6″). Saw them lengthwise, each
into three equal pieces. Plane one side
and one edge of each piece, then lay
them together with the heart-side up.
Compose an attractive pattern, placing heart-side against heart-side and
sapwood side against sapwood side.
Apply adhesive to all the joining
edges, glue the pieces together with
cramps, and allow to dry.

1

Cut the glued workpiece into two parts, about 350×1200 mm (14″×48″), and plane them to a thickness of about 20 mm (¾″). From them, cut two 900 mm (35″) lengths for the carcase's top and bottom, as well as four 10 cm (4″) pieces for the sides and partitions. Saw the partitions 6 mm (¼″) shorter, to leave room for the back of the case later on.

Draw the positions of the sides and partitions onto the top and bottom. Use an end-cutter to make grooves (a), with a depth of 5 mm (³⁄₁₆″), in the middle of each mark—but stop 20 mm (¾″) from the front edge.

2

Using the circular saw, cut tenons (a), about 5 mm (³⁄₁₆″) deep, on the sides and partitions. They should fit tightly into the grooves. Saw off about 22 mm (⅞″) from the tenons' fronts.

Mark notches (b) on the partitions, 30 mm (1³⁄₁₆″) from the carcase's rear edge, 10 mm (⅜″) deep and 21 mm (¹³⁄₁₆″) wide. Cut them out with the circular saw, aided by its mitre fence and rip fence.

Place the partitions in their grooves, and mark a groove (c) for the locking batten in the lid. Use the router to cut out this groove, 10×21 mm (⅜″×¹³⁄₁₆″). As a router guide, you can use a board fixed with cramps or short nails (see page 53).

3

Cut a batten (a), 20×9×350 mm (¾″×⅜″×13¾″), to fit in the routed groove. It should have a clearance of 1.5 mm (¹⁄₁₆″), so as not to jam in the groove.

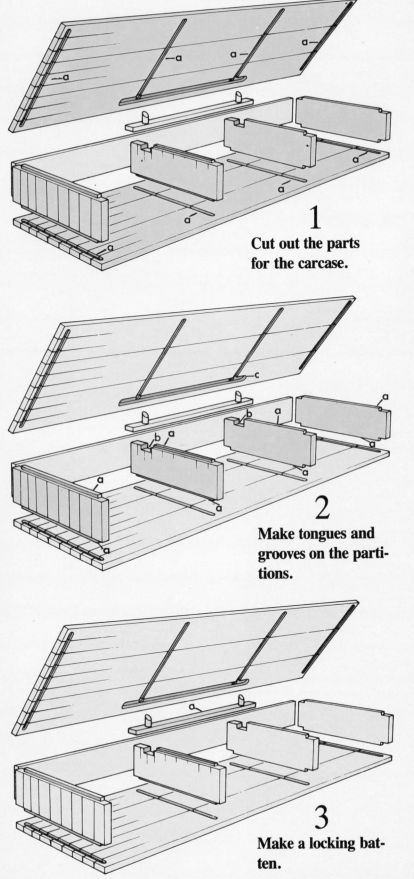

1

Cut out the parts for the carcase.

2

Make tongues and grooves on the partitions.

3

Make a locking batten.

4
Drill holes for the springs.

5
Make the mirror stands.

6
Cut the parts for the mirror case.

4

Drill holes (*a*) in the partitions' notches, about 40 mm (1⁹⁄₁₆″) deep and a little wider than the spiral springs you plan to use. Push the springs into the holes, and check that they can be compressed to fit entirely inside.

Place the partitions into the bottom piece, lay the batten in the notches, and mark where the springs meet the batten. At these points, use a 10 mm (³⁄₈″) drill to make holes (*b*) about 3 mm (¹⁄₈″) deep, as guides for the springs.

5

Cut two bits of wood, 40 mm high and 22×110 mm (1⁵⁄₈″×⁷⁄₈″×4³⁄₈″), to serve as mirror stands between the top of the drawer chest and the mirror case. The grain should run vertically.

6

The mirror case is to be made next. From a 25×150 mm (1″×6″) board, cut two lengths of 800 and 900 mm (31½″ and 35½″). Plane one edge, and plane one side down to 20 mm (¾″). Cut them lengthwise and glue them back together (see pages 65–67).

Using the circular saw, adjust the widths to 140 mm (5½″) plus one blade thickness. Then cut out two lengths of 340 mm (13³⁄₈″) and two of 400 mm (15¾″). Plane these down to 20 mm (¾″). They will be the case's sides, shown here as (*a*) and (*b*) respectively.

To form the grooves (*c*), mark at 20 mm (¾″) from the ends of the short sides. Adjust the circular saw to leave that distance between the rip fence and the blade's outer edge. Set the blade height at 11 mm (⁷⁄₁₆″). Cut the grooves along the marks, aided by the mitre fence. Then readjust to 10 mm (³⁄₈″) between the rip fence and the blade's inner edge, and cut again. Between these cuts, make several more to clean out the groove.

Saw out the tenons (*d*) on the long vertical sides. They should fit tightly into the grooves. The method is described on pages 112–113.

Smooth the interior of the case and glue it together with cramps.

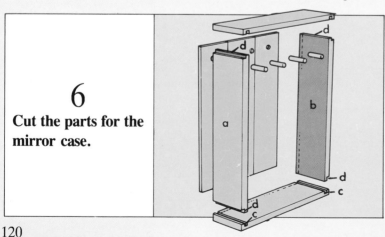

7

Adjust the rip fence so that there is 110 mm (4⅜″) between the saw blade's inner edge and the rip fence. Set the blade height at 22 mm (⅞″), and cut out the door frame. Mark one side so that the frame will not be turned wrongly when you mount the hinges.

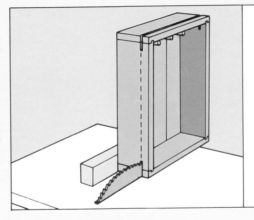

7
Saw off the door frame.

8

Cut out a rebate (a) for the mirror case's back, 6 mm (¼″) deep and 10 mm (⅜″) wide. Chisel the corners clean. Measure for a back piece, and saw it from 6 mm (¼″) plywood. Insert the back gently—otherwise the angle of the case may be changed in relation to the door frame. Do not fasten the back yet.

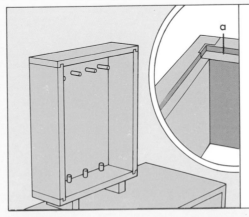

8
Rebate the back of the mirror case.

9

Mark the positions of the hinges, which are of the invisible Soss type, with their midpoints at one-sixth of the frame's height from the top and bottom edges.

To inset hinges of this type, a knot borer can be used. First make two shallow holes for fastening the plates. With a chisel, cut out the middle hole for the hinge pin.

Smooth and round off all the edges before mounting the hinges.

9
Inset and mount the hinges.

10

For the mirror frame, cut pieces 33 mm (1⁵⁄₁₆″) wide, from a board 25 mm (1″) thick. Plane one side and one edge to make them 30×20 mm (1⅛″×¾″). Cut them to 6 mm (¼″) shorter than the door frame's inner dimensions.

Make mortises in the vertical pieces and tenons on the shorter horizontal pieces (see pages 46–47).

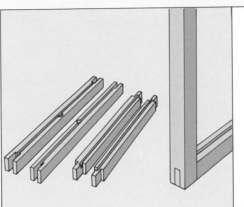

10
Make the parts for the mirror frame.

11

Assemble the frame and rebate it for the mirror glass.

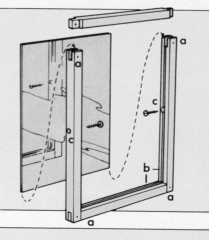

12

Drill the holes in the mirror stands.

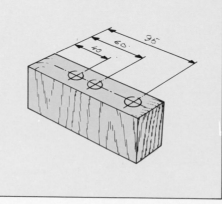

13

Drill matching holes in the bottom of the mirror case.

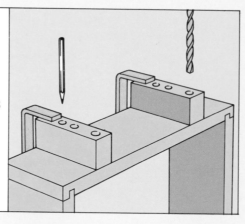

14

Drill corresponding holes in the carcase top and locking batten.

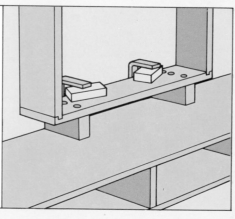

11

Fit the mirror frame together without gluing it. Bore a 3-mm (⅛″) hole (*a*) in each corner from the inside, and countersink it for a screw head. Mark the corners with numbers. Disassemble the frame and cut a groove (*b*) for the mirror glass, about 10 mm (⅜″) from the front edge, 3.5 mm (⅛″) wide and mm (³⁄₁₆″) deep. If you use the circular saw instead of a router, you can fill up the grooves in the frame's end-wood after the glass has been mounted.

For the mounting screws, drill hole (*c*) of diameter 5 mm (³⁄₁₆″) in each vertical side of the frame, 5 mm (³⁄₁₆″) under its midpoint.

12

Mark each of the two stand blocks at 40, 60 and 95 mm (1⁹⁄₁₆″, 2⅜″, 3¾″) measuring from the back edge. Drill a central hole 10 mm (⅜″) wide at each mark.

13

Mark 60 mm (2⅜″) in from the sides of the mirror-case's frame. Turn the case upside down. Fix the stand blocks in place with cramps. Using its middle and front holes as guides, drill a 10 mm (⅜″) hole through the frame.

Stick a pencil into the rear hole and mark the hole's center. This hole should be drilled with a 5 mm (³⁄₁₆″) drill.

14

Insert dowels into the middle and front holes, then loosen the cramps. Place the mirror frame and attached stand blocks on the drawer top, then tighten with clamps. Remove the dowels and drill through the middle and front holes with a 10 mm (⅜″) drill. Loosen the cramps and remove the mirror frame, leaving only the stand blocks on the top. Replace the dowels in the middle and front holes for guidance. Drill the rear holes right through the top and the locking batten with a 10 mm (⅜″) drill.

15

Prepare a long piece of dowelling 10 mm (⅜″) in diameter, of a hardwood such as birch. It should be about 300 mm (1′) long, to supply the locking pins and central dowels.

Cut two dowels (*a*) of length 62 mm (2⅜″). Divide each in the middle at an angle of 30°. Glue one half into the hole in the locking batten. Make sure that the angled faces of these halves are parallel. To ensure that the locking pins will move easily, widen the rear holes with a 10.5 mm (⁷⁄₁₆″) drill.

Now the drawer carcase can be glued together, using band cramps and tension blocks. At the same time, fit the locking batten. Avoid getting glue into the openings for the spiral springs and locking batten.

16

Measure the openings for the three drawers. Cut three lengths of wood to provide the front, back, and side pieces. Plane one side and one edge to a thickness of 20 mm (¾″). Adjust the width to exactly equal the carcase's inner height. Cut the pieces according to the measurements, but make the drawers less deep by 8 mm (⁵⁄₁₆″) to leave room for the back of the carcase.

17

Mark the dovetails in the drawer front and back pieces. Cut them with a tenon saw and clean them out with a chisel (see pages 92–93).

18

Mark dovetail joints in all the drawer side pieces, and cut them with the tenon saw (see page 92).

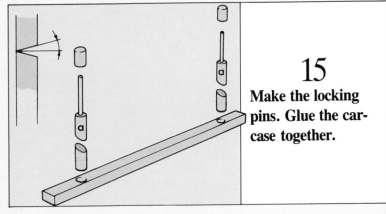

15

Make the locking pins. Glue the carcase together.

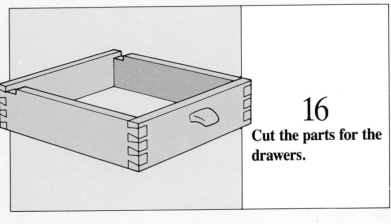

16

Cut the parts for the drawers.

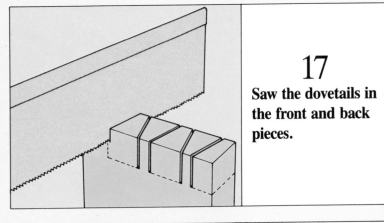

17

Saw the dovetails in the front and back pieces.

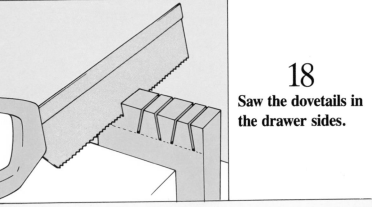

18

Saw the dovetails in the drawer sides.

19
Cut grooves for the drawer bottoms.

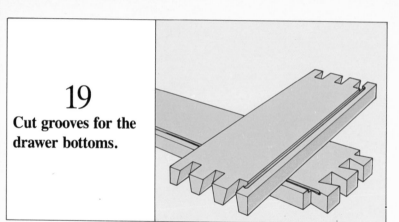

19

Cut grooves for the bottoms in all the drawer pieces, about 5 mm (³⁄₁₆″) from their lower edges. Remember to stop cutting 10 mm (³⁄₈″) before the ends of the pieces.

20
Assemble and glue the drawers.

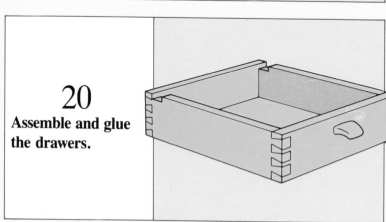

20

Cut the bottoms from 6 mm (¼″) plywood. Smooth the bottoms and all inner sides, and check that the drawers are squared, before gluing them together. Plane the drawers so that they slide easily, with a tiny fraction of clearance all round.

21
Shape and mount the drawer handles.

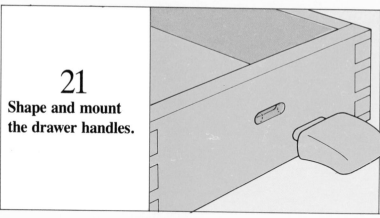

21

Smooth the drawer fronts and round off all corners and edges. For the handles, drill two holes 10 mm (³⁄₈″) wide, 15 mm (⁹⁄₁₆″) apart, and 30 mm (1³⁄₁₆″) from the upper edge of each drawer. Enlarge these with a chisel. Cut and shape the handles according to taste. Saw their tenons and glue them into the enlarged holes.

22
Notch the drawers to take the locking batten.

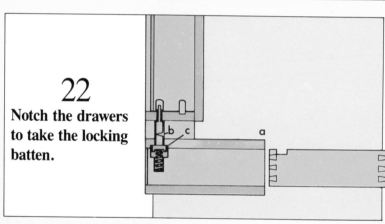

22

Measure the depth from the carcase's front edge (*a*) to the locking batten (*b*). To show where the notch (*c*) for the batten will be, place the drawers together, measure the same depth from their front edges, and mark across the tops of their sides.

Then use the circular saw to cut the notches at the mark. Check that the drawers lock, by inserting them into the carcase and pushing down the locking batten. It should fit in the notches and hold the drawers in. Ultimately, the drawers will lock or unlock because the spring-loaded batten moves down or up when you turn its angle-cut pins, the secret behind the tilting mirror!

23

Cut a rebate for the carcase back, 6 mm (¼″) deep and 10 mm (⅖″) wide, using a router with rebating cutter. Fit the plywood back. Smooth the outside and round off corners and edges.

24

Before mounting the mirror case, finish the locking device (picture 13). Make two knobs (*a*) and two brass pins (*b*), the latter 5 mm (³⁄₁₆″) in diameter and 55 mm (2³⁄₁₆″) long. Using a 5 mm (³⁄₁₆″) drill, make a central hole in the knobs, and another of depth 20 mm (¾″) in the angle-cut pins (*c*). Glue the brass pins into the angle-cut pins with epoxy adhesive.

Attach the mirror case's back piece with 20 mm (¾″) panel pins. Insert the angle-cut pins and glue on the mirror case, fixing it with the four through-going dowels.

Use epoxy adhesive again to glue on the two locking knobs. Do not pour much glue in the bored holes of the knobs, or it will run down and spoil the whole locking device.

25

Assemble the mirror frame with its glass. Screw it to the door frame with two round-headed screws.

Finishing

Treat all parts with plastic varnish. Dull them with steel wool of grade 0.

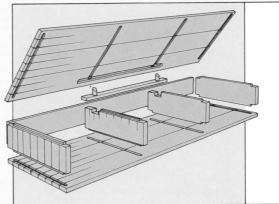

23
Make and fit the carcase back.

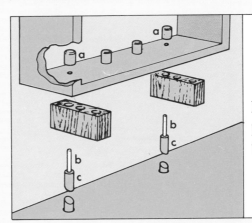

24
Make the locking pins. Fit the back of the mirror case.

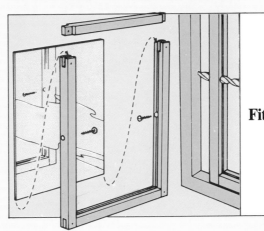

25
Fit the mirror glass.

ROCKING HORSE

MATERIAL
softwood or hardwood

TOOLS
planer
bandsaw
circular saw
router
hand drill
marking gauge
bevel gauge

Constructional drawing
The measurements suggested can be adopted, or may be adjusted as convenient. The key to this particular construction is that the legs are angled in two directions, sidewise and longitudinally (angles X and Y in the constructional drawing). They must be slanted in such a way that the rockers are located outside the vertical line of the seat; the horse will then be stable.

Preparation
Start by cutting pieces to make the seat. They should be about 37 mm (1½″) thick initially. Cut them into lengths about 50 mm (2″) wide, and plane on one side and both edges.

Glue the pieces together with the heart side uppermost (see pages 65-66). When the adhesive has dried, plane and cut to the desired length. Draw the shape of the seat, and mark the length of the groove for fastening the head.

1

Use the router to make the groove (*a*) into which the head of the horse is to be fastened. Note that the guide (*b*) should be fitted on the correct side of the router so that it can work against the direction of rotation. The groove should be 12–15 mm (about ½″) deep.

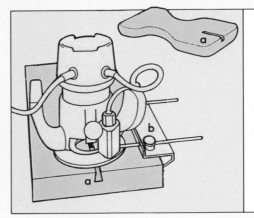

1

Cut the groove in the seat piece.

2

Cut out the shape of the seat with the bandsaw. Remember to lower the blade guard (*a*) so that the minimum amount of blade is exposed.

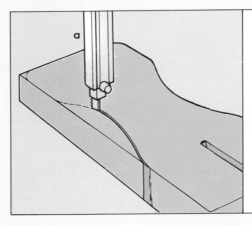

2

Cut out the shape of the seat.

3

Round off the edge of the seat with the router. Use a suitably sized cutter with a guide.

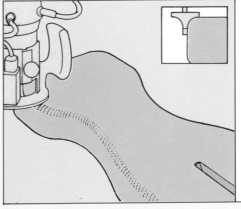

3

The router is used to give the seat a comfortable edge.

4

For the laminated rockers, cut several thin knot-free slats which are 100 mm (4″) longer and 5 mm (³⁄₁₆″) wider than the final measurements. They should be about 5 mm (³⁄₁₆″) thick when planed.

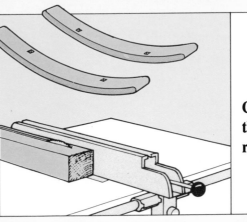

4

Cut slats to make the laminated rockers.

127

5

Make a template for gluing the rockers and bending them.

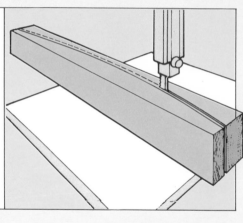

5

Cut a piece of planed timber, slightly wider than the rocker, which has to be glued into a curved shape. Mark the curve of the rocker on the piece of wood, using a thin slat or steel ruler bent into the desired shape.

Cut carefully along the line, using a bandsaw (see picture). Then measure the total thickness of the rocker slats, set the marking gauge, and mark another curve on the piece that will be the male mould by moving the gauge along the previously cut edge. Cut on the correct side of this line.

6

Glue the rocker slats and cut the rocker to the desired width.

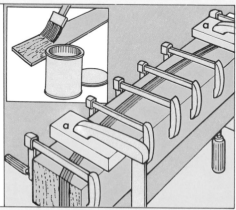

6

Glue the slats together with an adhesive of the phenolic resin type. Apply the adhesive to the slats, place paper between the gluing template and the slats, then bend them into shape in the template by cramping it together — start from the middle and work towards the ends. If the slats threaten to slide sideways, secure two pieces of wood (*a*) on each side of the rocker, having first placed a piece of paper between the surfaces. Allow to dry.

Plane one of the edges of the rocker, then trim to the required width with the circular saw.

7

Cut to size and plane pieces of wood for the legs and rails. The legs will be cut down later.

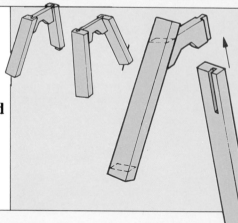

7

Cut pieces (23×50 mm, $^{15}/_{16}''×2''$) for the four legs and add a further 100 mm (4'') per leg. Cut and plane two pieces for the rails, about 23 mm ($1^{15}/_{16}''$) thick.

Cut the legs at right angles at one end. They will be joined in pairs by the rails.

8

Make a groove for the rail in each leg.

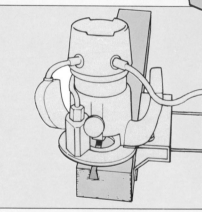

8

Mark and cut the grooves for the rails in the four legs.

9

Before the rails are cut to size, measure the angle X between the legs and the seat with a bevel gauge on the constructional drawing, and transfer the angle to the mitre fence of the circular saw. Cut the rails to the correct size, including the tenons.

Using the groove that has already been cut in a leg as a template, mark the dimensions of the tenons on the rails. Cut the tenons with the circular saw if the blade can be angled, or use the router. Make a sample tenon using an off-cut from the rail, in order to test the fit.

10

Mark the shape of the rails on the pieces already cut (see step 7) and use the bandsaw for cutting.

Drill the screw holes (*a*) in each rail. Countersink the holes until only about 25 mm (1″) of the hole remains (the screws should be 50 mm/2″ long). Glue the rails and the legs together to form pairs of legs. Allow to dry.

11

The second angle, Y, of the legs (see constructional drawing) must now be cut. Place the rail against the rip fence, and set the mitre fence to the first angle of the leg (X°). Remove the rip fence. Set the blade at angle Y, and trim off the surplus parts of the legs and rail.

Saw off the legs at the other end so that they are the same length.

12

Screw the pairs of legs in place under the seat.

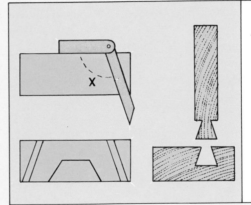

9

Cut the rails and their tenons at the sidewise angle.

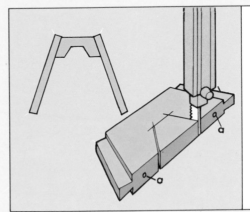

10

Cut the shape of the rails, then glue the rails to the legs.

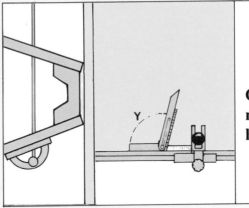

11

Cut the legs and rails at the longitudinal angle.

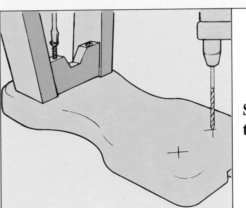

12

Screw the legs onto the seat.

13

Mark the curve of the rocker on each leg, and cut the legs.

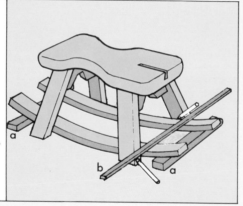

14

Drill holes in the rockers at the points where they are to be fastened to the legs.

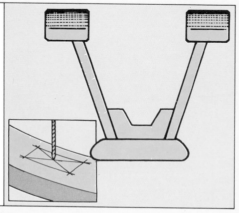

15

Drill holes through both the rockers and the temporarily attached legs.

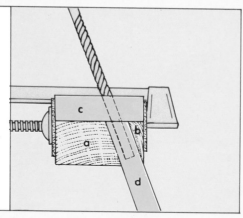

16

Fasten the rockers to the legs by means of dowels and glue, and cut the rockers to length.

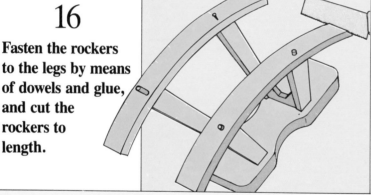

13

Stand the whole thing on a level surface, and place the rockers against the insides of the legs. In order to get the rockers parallel, use two pieces of wood (*a*) placed at right angles under them. When they are in the correct position, trace the outline of the upper edge of the rocker on the inside of each leg. Next, place a thin batten (*b*) across the rockers and trace the bottom edge of the batten onto the edges of the legs.

Cut along the marked lines with a coping saw.

14

Stand the seat with its legs upwards, and place the rockers on the legs. Smooth the legs' ends if needed. When they fit, mark the locations for the legs on the rockers, and also mark the centre point of each location by drawing diagonals across the four corners of the leg's outlines.

Use a 2 mm (1/16″) drill for making holes through the rockers in the centre of the outlines. Each rocker is then fastened to its leg by means of a 50 mm (2″) nail driven through the hole. Do not hammer the nails fully home.

15

Cut two pieces of wood (*a*, *b*) so that their combined width and that of the leg is equal to the width of the rocker (*c*). Place these pieces on the rocker, one on each side of the leg (*d*), and secure with a cramp. Remove the nail and use a 12 mm (1/2″) drill bit to make a hole through the rocker and about 25 mm (1″) up into the leg. Use a portable drill.

16

Take a length of dowel and press it into the drilled hole: it will be trimmed later after gluing. Remove the nail from the next hole, and fasten the leg to the rocker as described above before drilling the next hole.

Decide the length of the rockers, mark the length of one rocker, and transfer it onto the other one. Cut the rockers to the correct length.

Smooth all surfaces and round off the edges and ends of the rockers, then glue them to the legs.

When the adhesive has dried, trim the dowel ends and smooth down.

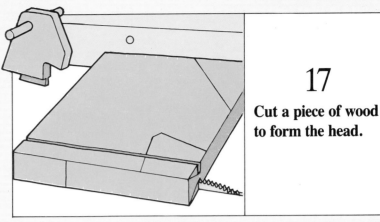

17

Cut a suitable piece of planed wood, and draw the shape of the head onto it. Cut the base of the neck so that the head is slanted forwards at the desired angle. Cut the shoulder of the tenon with the circular saw.

17

Cut a piece of wood to form the head.

18

Cut out the tenon so that it fits into the groove (see picture). The angle of the saw blade (*a*) is determined by the angle of the routing cutter (*b*) which made the groove in the seat (see step 1).

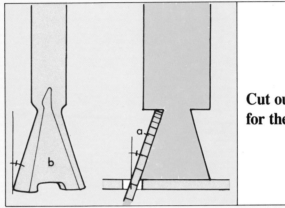

18

Cut out the tenon for the head.

19

Cut out the head of the horse with the bandsaw and drill a 20 mm (¾″) hole for the handlebar. Cut a length of dowelling of the same diameter. Smooth down the head and dowelling.

Place the bar in position, and make a mark on each side of the head. Then pull the bar out until both markings are visible on one side of the head. Apply adhesive to half the surface and press the handle back into position.

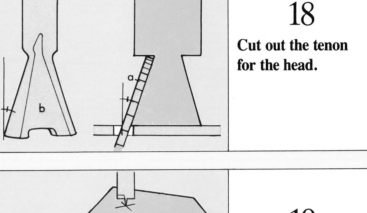

19

Cut out the horse's head and place the handlebar in a hole through the head.

20

Glue the head onto the seat.

Finishing
Use polyurethane varnish or transparent glaze.

20

Glue the head onto the seat before applying the finish.

LOOM

Preparation

Start by cutting to size

  2 pieces 500 mm (19¾″) long
    from 20×125 mm (¾″×5″) timber
  1 piece 800 mm (31½″) long
    from the same wood
  1 piece 500 mm (19¾″), 25 mm
    (1″) thick, and any width
  1 piece 300×15×35 mm
    (11¾″×⅝″×1⅜″)
  1 piece 320 mm (12⅝″) from
    20×75 mm (¾″×3″) timber

These are for beams, heddle bars, shed rods, and frame rails.

Plane one side and one edge on all the pieces.

Plane the pieces that are 20 mm (¾″) thick down to 15 mm (⅝″) and the pieces that are 25 mm (1″) down to 23 mm (⅞″). Cut the pieces parallel, using the circular saw.

MATERIAL
birch or beech
iron wire 2 mm (¹⁄₁₆″)
  in diameter

TOOLS
planer
circular saw
pillar drill
power drill
tenon saw or bandsaw

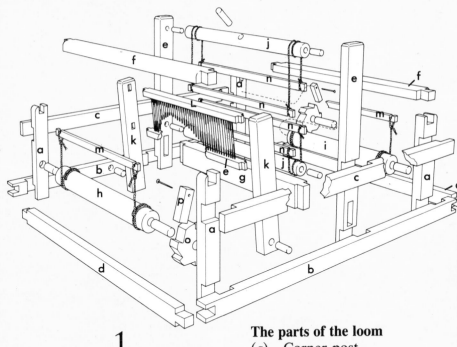

The parts of the loom

- (a) Corner post
- (b) Lower side rail
- (c) Central side rail
- (d) Front rail/back rail
- (e) Centre post
- (f) Top cross rail
- (g) Centre cross rail
- (h) Cloth beam
- (i) Warp beam
- (j) Heddle-bar beam
- (k) Reed side frame
- (l) Reed cross rail
- (m) Shed rod
- (n) Heddle bar
- (o) Catchwheel
- (p) Catch

1

Cut one of the pieces that you have planed to 15 mm (⅝″) to a length of exactly 480 mm (18⅞″). This will form the two lower side rails and the two central side rails on the long side.

Mark the cut-outs for the halving joints which should be half the thickness of the rails. Start by drawing a line 15 mm (⅝″) from each end.

Then measure 190 mm (7½″) from the rear end of the piece and draw another line all the way across. The width of the cut-outs should be 25 mm (1″). Mark the cut-out according to these measurements.

2

Adjust the height of the circular saw blade to half the thickness of the wood, i.e. 7.5 mm (⁵⁄₁₆″). Make a trial cut in a piece of scrap wood 15 mm (⅝″) thick, then turn it over and make another cut, so that the second one just touches the first, cutting the wood in two.

(*Picture*) First make the outer cuts. Then cut the intermediate section by moving the piece cut by cut, a blade width at a time with the help of the mitre guide.

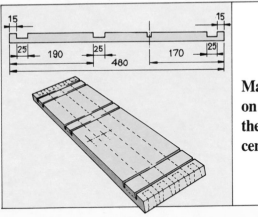

1

Mark up the joints on the workpiece for the lower and central side rails.

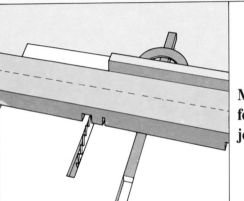

2

Make the cut-outs for the halving joints.

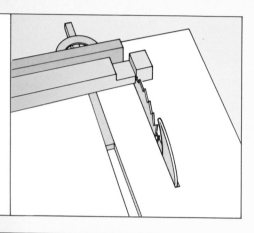

3

Saw the workpiece into the rails and mark for the reed joint.

4

Cut sockets in the lower side rails for the front rails.

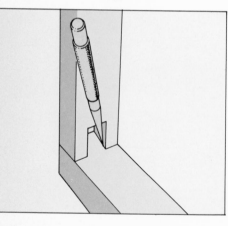

5

Cut tails in the front rail for the sockets on the lower side rails.

6

Make joints on the posts. Make tails on the top cross rails.

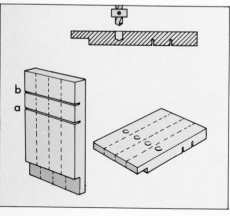

3

Cut the wood into four 25 mm (1″) wide rails. The two lower side rails should be 480 mm (18⅞″) long (equal to the length of the wood), and the two central side rails 450 mm (17¾″) long. The pieces for the two central side rails should thus be shortened by 15 mm (⅝″) at each end.

Make a mark in the centre of the insides of the lower side rails, 170 mm (6¹¹⁄₁₆″) from the front end for a 10 mm (⅜″) hole to take the rounded axle of the reed's side frame.

4

Transfer the thickness of the front rail onto the lower side rail with a marking gauge. Measure the width of the end-wood and divide it by four. Mark this distance in from either end. Use the bevel gauge to draw a line at 10° from the two marks across the end-wood. Continue the lines down to the socket shoulder.

Saw and clean out the sockets as on pages 92–93.

5

Take the other piece of wood that is 500 mm (19¾″) long and planed to a thickness of 15 mm (⅝″), and cut off a piece 240 mm (9⅞″) long. Then divide this into 4 pieces, 15×25 mm (⅝″×1″). Keep two pieces for step 6.

Place the cut-out sockets on the lower side rails against the ends of the front rail and mark the tails. Number each socket and tail so you don't mix them up later on. Saw and cut out the tails as on pages 92–93. Repeat for the back rail.

6

Using the remaining part of the 500 mm (19¾″) long piece, prepare the wood for the four corner posts, 15×25 mm (⅝″×1″).

Make a mark 25 mm (1″) from one end for the cut-out of the halving joint. Then measure and mark from the same end 120 mm (4¾″) (*a*) and 145 mm (5¾″) (*b*). Draw a line all the way across the wood at these markings, and make the cut-outs by repeatedly sawing with the circular saw. Then rip-cut the piece to make the four corner posts.

Finally, mark a point in the centre of the corner post and 60 mm (2⅜″) from its bottom end. Drill a 10 mm (⅜″) hole for the axles of the cloth beam and the warp beam, but do not drill right through. Use a stoppered drill.

Mark and cut out sockets in the tops of the four corner posts, as in step 4.

7

Now take the two 15×25 mm (⅝″×1″) pieces for the top cross rails, left over from step 5, and mark up and cut the tails, as you did in step 5.

Mark which ends belong together.

8

Now make the centre posts from the wood prepared at the start (measuring 320×15×75 mm, or 12⅝″×⅝″×3″).

First mark the cut-outs for the lower side rails (*a*) and for the central side rails (*b*), using a corner post as a template. Then mark the mortise (*c*) for the centre cross rail 35 mm (1⅜″) from the bottom of the post, 35 mm (1⅜″) high and 10 mm (⅜″) wide. Finally, mark two holes on the wood (*d, e*) for the axles of the two heddle-bar beams.

Make the cut-outs with the circular saw.

9

Drill the mortise using a pillar drill fitted with a 10 mm (⅜″) bit. As a guide, use a batten nailed to a piece of chipboard which is then fastened to the platform of the pillar drill. First drill the outer holes and then the intermediate ones. Move the wood backwards and forwards in the drill so as to remove most of the wood from the hole. (*Continued over*)

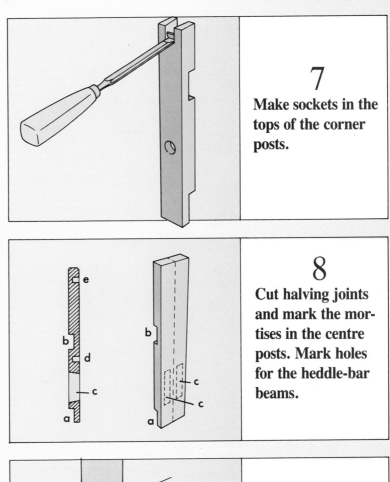

7
Make sockets in the tops of the corner posts.

8
Cut halving joints and mark the mortises in the centre posts. Mark holes for the heddle-bar beams.

9
Cut the mortises in the centre posts using a specially made drill jig.

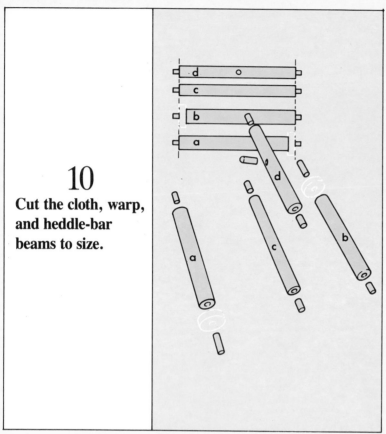

10
Cut the cloth, warp, and heddle-bar beams to size.

Use a chisel to cut out the corners. Drill two holes for the axles of the heddle-bar beams. Do not drill right through but stop about 4 mm (³⁄₁₆″) short.

Take the piece prepared for the centre cross rail at the beginning (300×15×35 mm, or 6″×⅝×1⅜″) and cut to its final size (240 mm, or 9⁷⁄₁₆″). Take the centre posts and mark up tenons, using the mortises as templates. Cut out the tenons as on page 47.

10
THE MOVING PARTS

The cloth beam (*a*) and the warp beam (*b*) should be 200 mm (7⅞″) long and 25 mm (1″) in diameter. The two heddle-bar beams (*c*, *d*) should also be 25 mm in diameter but 210 mm (8¼″) long. They can most easily be made from a piece of dowel 25 mm (1″) in diameter.

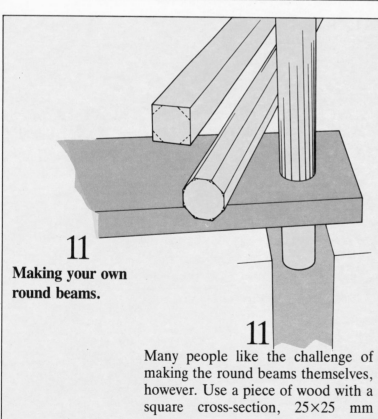

11
Making your own round beams.

Many people like the challenge of making the round beams themselves, however. Use a piece of wood with a square cross-section, 25×25 mm (1″×1″) and 850 mm (33½″) long. First reduce the square to an octagon, then to sixteen sides. This is most easily done by using the circular saw with a blade angled at 45° to saw the wood into an octagon. Then plane it down to sixteen sides.

If a circular saw is not available, use the plane for both processes.

Adjust the plane to a fine cut and plane the wood all over. Then drill a 23 mm (⅞″) hole in a piece of beech or some other hardwood. Use a mallet to drive the dowel through the hole, and then smooth down with fine abrasive paper. The result is a 850 mm (33½″) long piece of dowelling with a diameter of 23 mm (⅞″), which is only slightly thinner than bought dowelling.

Cut the beams from the dowel, two of 200 mm (7⅞″) and two of 210 mm (8¼″).

12

Now drill holes in the centre of the ends of the four beams. This is most easily done by first drilling a hole with the pillar drill in the centre of a 50 mm (2″) long block which is 23×23 mm (⅞″×⅞″). Fasten block and beam to the work-bench with some wood between them and cramp in such a way that the hole is adjacent to the centre of the beam. Drill with a power drill through the square block and about 20 mm (¾″) into the end of the beam.

13
CATCHWHEELS

You need two catchwheels for the loom. Take a piece of plywood 10 mm (⅜″) thick and 55 mm (1⅛″) wide. Draw a square on it, 55×55 mm (2⅛″×2⅛″) and join the diagonals. Adjust a pair of compasses to a radius of 27.5 mm (1¹⁄₁₆″) and draw a circle.

Divide up the circumference, using the radius measurement to give six points (A1–A6) along the circumference, equidistant from each other. Draw a line from each of these points to the centre of the circle (A). Measure 5 mm (³⁄₁₆″) from A1 and mark the point (B1), and repeat for A2–A6.

Adjust the compasses and draw a circle from the same central point but with a radius of 20 mm (¾″). Draw a line from B1 to the intersection between A–A1 and the inner circle. Do the same between B2 and the intersection of A–A2 and the inner circle, etc., thus drawing all the cogs for the catchwheel.

14

Cut out all the cogs with a tenon saw or a bandsaw. Drill a 10 mm (⅜″) hole in the centre with the pillar drill.

Make dowelling 10 mm (⅜″) in diameter in the same way as the beams were made (or simply buy 10 mm dowelling at the timber-yard). The dowelling should be enough for all the

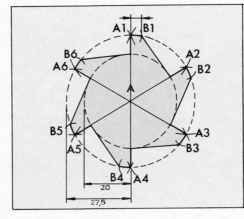

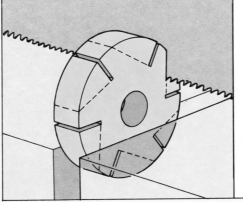

12
Drill centred holes in the ends of the four beams.

13
Mark up the catchwheels.

14
Cut out the catchwheel cogs, fit them with dowels, and attach them.

axles, which means that a total length of about 450 mm (18″) is needed.

Cut eight axles for the holes drilled in the beams and glue them in. Adjust the protruding part to a length of 10 mm (⅜″).

Glue on the catchwheels to the dowels of the cloth and warp beams, making sure that their direction is the same as in the picture.

15

Assemble and glue together the side frames of the loom.

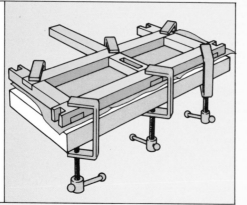

15

Glue together the side frames of the loom. Use a piece of chipboard as a support and tighten carefully with cramps.

16

Round off the top edges of the top cross rails.

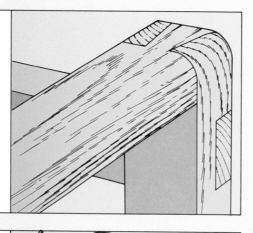

16

Before gluing the loom together, round off the upper edge of the top cross rails so that warp and cloth can run freely—see the inset picture in the top right-hand corner. The rounding should be considerable, with a radius of 10 mm (⅜″).

Drill a 10 mm (⅜″) hole in the middle of the top heddle-bar beam. Glue in a 30 mm (1⅛″) piece of dowelling to act as a lever.

17

Glue the loom carcase together.

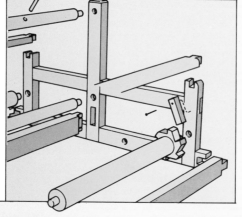

17

Assemble the loom without glue. Check that all parts move freely.

Glue together the frame, and check the diagonals. Tighten carefully using sash cramps. Note that the beams should not be glued but remain movable.

18

Make and fit catches for the catchwheels.

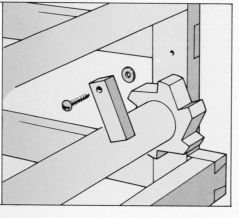

18

Cut two catches for the catchwheels 10×10 mm (⅜″×⅜″) and 30 mm (1⅛″) long. Drill a hole for a round-headed screw, and place a thin washer in between. The catch should move so easily that it falls from its own weight.

19

Cut wood to length for two shed rods and four heddle bars, 6×12 mm (¼"×½")—they look exactly the same. Cut them 15 mm (⅝") shorter than the inside measurement of the loom, i.e. 210 – 15 mm = 195 mm (8¼"–⅝" = 7⅝").

Cut a small groove about 10 mm (⅜") from the ends of all the rods and bars. The groove should be 3 mm (⅛") in order to take the cord.

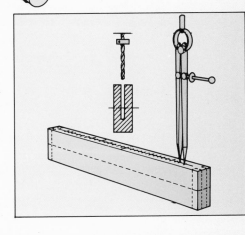

19

Make the shed rods and che four heddle bars.

20

The assembly of the beams, shed rods, and heddle bars.

21

Make the top and bottom cross rails for the reed and drill them with holes.

20

The picture shows the heddle-bar beams, the cloth and warp beams, shed rods and heddle bars, joined together by lengths of cord.

21
THE REED

To make the reed cross rails, use a piece of wood measuring 25×10 mm (1"×⅜") and mark the inside measurement of the loom minus 15 mm (210–15 = 195 mm, i.e. 8¼"–⅝" = 7⅝"). This allows enough extra wood to make the tenons.

Use a pair of compasses to mark points at 3 mm (⅛") intervals for about 75 mm (3") in both directions from the middle, along a centre line drawn on the top edge, which is 25 mm (1") wide. Drill 18 mm (¹¹⁄₁₆") deep holes very carefully (use a stopper) with a 2 mm (¹⁄₁₆") bit.

Cut the wood lengthwise along the middle to obtain two pieces equally long and wide, one of them drilled through, the other drilled to a depth of 7 mm (⁹⁄₃₂").

22
Make the end pieces for the reed side frame.

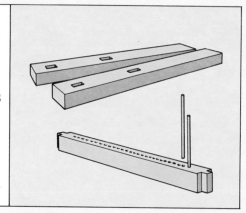

23
Round the base of the reed frame. Glue the reed together.

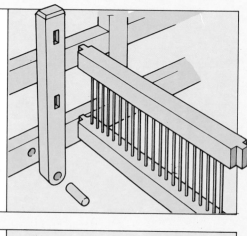

24
Make the shuttle.

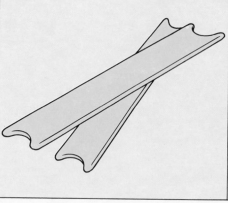

22

Cut two end pieces for the reed side frame, 250 mm (10″) long and 25×15 mm (1″×⅝″). Mark out mortises 15 mm and 110 mm (⅝″ and 4⅝″) from one end, then drill the holes with a 6 mm (¼″) bit and trim them with a chisel.

Cut tenons (6×12 mm, ¼″×½″) at the ends of the drilled reed cross rails.

Cut 2 mm (1/16″) straightened iron wire into lengths of 105 mm (4⅛″) and press them into the holes that have not been drilled right through the wood.

Fit the other ends of the wire into the corresponding holes in the cross rail that has been drilled through. Press together to get the correct distance for the tenons so that they fit exactly into the mortises.

23

Round the bases of both sides of the reed frame considerably (radius 12.5 mm, ½″). Drill a 10 mm (⅜″) hole right through at the base of both the sides.

Glue the reed together, using cramps.

When the glue has dried, assemble the reed into the loom by pressing axles through the frame ends and into the pre-drilled holes in the lower side rails. Only glue the axles in the holes in the frame ends.

24
THE SHUTTLE

The shuttle should be as thin as possible (about 3×25 mm and about 150 mm long, i.e. ⅛″×1″ and 6″ long) with a notch at each end for winding on the weft.

Smooth down the shuttle carefully and round off all edges to prevent it from getting stuck in the warp.

Finishing
Give the entire loom a coat of varnish.

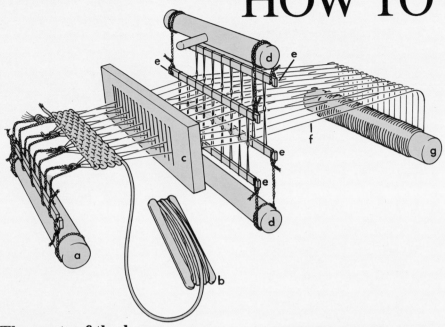

The parts of the loom

(*a*) The cloth beam rolls up the finished cloth.

(*b*) The shuttle carries the weft thread.

(*c*) The reed keeps the warp threads separate and parallel, and beats the weft against the shed of the cloth.

(*d*) The upper and lower heddle-bar beams hold the heddle bars, and the upper bar causes the warp to cross to make a new shed after each weft is beaten in.

(*e*) Heddle bars.

(*f*) Warp. This comprises the warp threads when mounted in the loom.

(*g*) The warp beam holds the warp rolled up, and releases it as it is required.

Weaving is a method of producing cloth on a loom from two sets of threads. One set runs through the length of the cloth and is called the warp. The other runs across the cloth and is called the weft. The reed beats the weft into the warp.

The weaving technique described here, in which every other warp thread is alternately threaded through a front and back heddle, is called two-leaved twill.

1

Make as many heddles as there are spacings in the reed. Heddles are most easily tied with a heddle jig, as shown. The jig is made from a piece of wood (*a*) which you drill as shown and fit with dowels. The outer dowels (*b*) give the heddles a constant length, while the inner, finer dowels (*c*) produce the heddle eye (*d*) in exactly the same place on all the heddles.

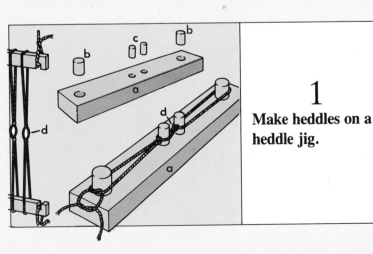

1
Make heddles on a heddle jig.

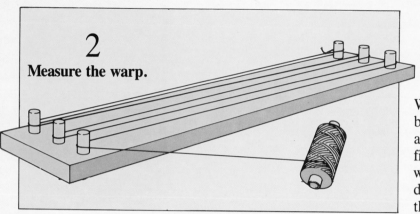

2
Measure the warp.

2

Wind the warp thread on a warp board, which you make from a suitable piece of wood which you drill and fit with dowels. Remember that the wood should always be smoothed down with abrasive paper, so that the thread does not snag on it.

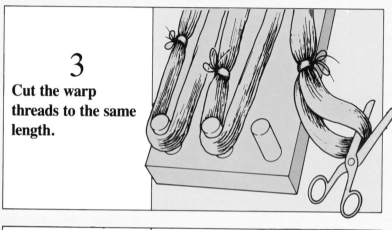

3
Cut the warp threads to the same length.

3

Tie the ends of the warp thread securely before cutting them. You now have a supply of warp threads, all of them the same length.

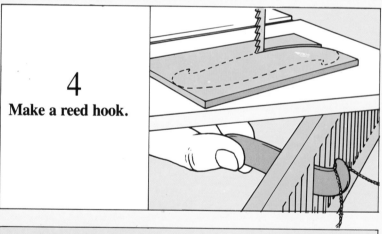

4
Make a reed hook.

4

Make a reed hook from a very thin piece of wood that you cut from a plank with the circular saw. Cut out the shape with a bandsaw or a fretsaw. Smooth it to a very fine finish.

Use the reed hook to draw the warp thread through the reed spacings.

5

Thread the first warp thread (*a1*) through the first spacing in the reed (*b*), through the first heddle eye in the front heddle group (*c1*, *c2*, etc.), and tie it to the shed rod (*d*).

Take the second warp thread (*a2*) and thread it through the second spacing in the reed, and through the first thread eyelet of the back heddle group (*e1*, etc.), and tie it to the shed rod.

Continue thus until you have threaded a warp thread through each spacing in the reed. Tie the shed rod to the warp beam (*f*).

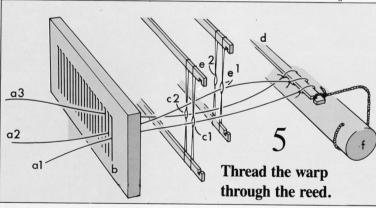

5
Thread the warp through the reed.

6

Grasp all the loose thread ends firmly in one hand and pull tight, so that they are equally taut. Have someone wind the warp beam for you, so that the warp thread is rolled up on the warp beam, while you keep a uniform tension on all the threads. If you are alone, secure the loom to the worktop with cramps, and wind the warp beam with your other hand.

Stop when the ends of the warp thread that you have in your hand are about 200 mm (8″) from the reed.

6

Pull the warp taut and wind it on the warp beam.

7

Tie the warp threads in groups of four to six threads, as shown. Then thread a piece of string through the warp groups and round the cloth beam's shed rod (*a*). Adjust the string until the tension is the same on all the warp threads.

Tie the shed rod to the cloth beam. The warp is now set up.

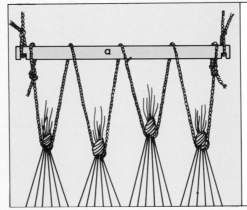

7

Tie the warp to the shed rod.

8

Tie the weft (yarn or strips of fabric in the colour you want) to the shuttle and pass it through the shed (the angle between the two sets of warp threads). Don't pull tightly. Simply lay the weft loosely in place, otherwise the edges of the finished fabric will pull in towards the middle. Pull the reed towards you to beat in the weft.

Now grasp the handle on the top heddle-bar beam and push it away from you, thus revolving the beam a half revolution, lowering the first group of heddles and raising the other group. This changes the shed of the warp and "locks" the first weft in place.

Continue the procedure until you have come as close as comfortable to the reed. Then turn the cloth beam to wind up the woven cloth, thus giving yourself more warp and more room in which to manoeuvre the shuttle.

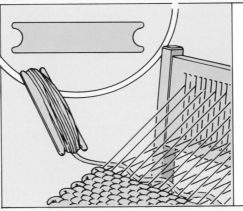

8

Pass the shuttle through the shed. Beat in the weft.

When you have woven the length of fabric that you had planned, cut off the warp threads and tie them back on the last weft, so that the fabric does not begin to unravel.

BRIEFCASE

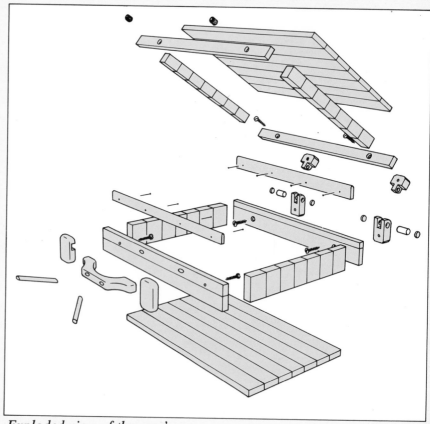

Exploded view of the case's construction.

MATERIAL
pine or any of the hardwoods, such as teak
thin metal rod
Teflon washers

TOOLS
circular saw
band saw
planer
pillar drill
belt sander
hacksaw
holed metal plate

1

Cut strips for the case's sides, top and bottom from a 12×100 mm (½″×4″) plank. If you use pine, the strip should be about 10 mm (⅜″) thick. If you use teak, the boards can be thinner, about 8 mm (⁵⁄₁₆″). Start by sawing them into lengths equal to the case's sides plus a bit extra. Then saw the strips into the desired width. Plane the surfaces and the edges.

Glue the strips together in one long piece from which the sides and the top and bottom of the case will be sawn later. Lay the strips together so that, as with all the other gluing sequences shown earlier, sapwood joins with sapwood, and heartwood with heartwood. If the wood has a distinctive grain, make an attractive pattern from it. Allow the glue to dry.

2

Using the circular saw, cut the glued piece in the middle, at exactly right angles. Then saw the outer edges straight. Turn the workpiece so that the saw is working lengthwise and saw off the two pieces for the top and bottom of the case.

3

The ends of the case are cut from endwood, to give the impression that the whole case comes from one block of wood. Cut the pieces, each with exactly the same thickness, from a suitable plank.

4

Glue the pieces together in a suitable pattern, with one of the edges pressed against a straight batten. This will make it easier to saw the piece into two identical parts. Allow to dry.

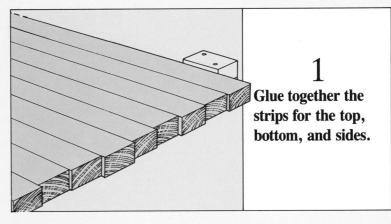

1
Glue together the strips for the top, bottom, and sides.

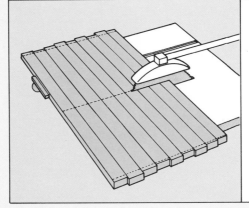

2
Saw the glued workpiece into the top, bottom and sides.

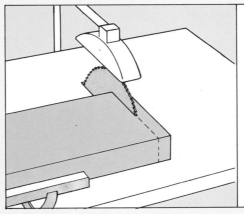

3
Saw the pieces for the two ends of the case.

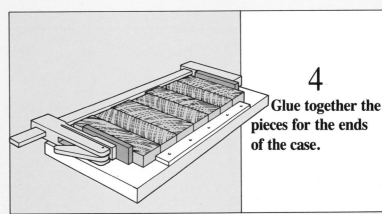

4
Glue together the pieces for the ends of the case.

5
Cut off the two end-pieces.

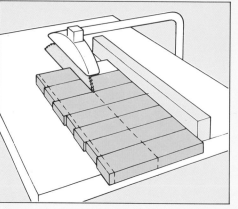

5

Mark the uneven edge of the glued end-pieces with a straight line and then mark up a line that divides the rest into two equal parts, the width of the case. Saw along the marked lines.

6
Make the grooves and tongues.

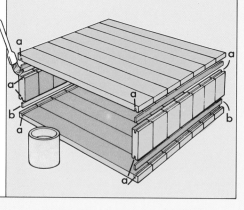

6

All the main parts of the case are now cut to size.

Using the circular saw, cut a groove (*a*) in each piece. As the grooves are to take tongues (*b*) that will join the parts together, you must make sure that each groove is exactly opposite and aligned to its mate.

Cut thin lathes of wood, as tongues for the grooves.

Spread wood adhesive on the tongues and in the grooves.

7
Cramp the side-pieces to the end-pieces.

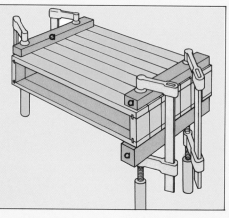

7

Fit the tongues into the grooves so that the two side-pieces are joined to the two end-pieces. Clamp them together, as shown. Remember to protect the surface of the case by placing cushion-blocks of wood (*a*) between the cramps and the surface. Allow to dry.

8
Glue the top-piece and the bottom-piece in position.

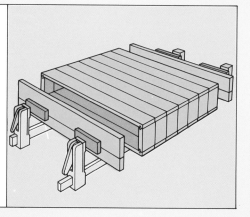

8

Glue the top-piece and the bottom-piece in position on the case. Use sash cramps. You now have a completely sealed box.

9

Give the case a smooth surface with a sander. Then set the blade on the circular saw at an angle of 45° and bevel the edges of the case. Rub down the bevelled edges to a smooth surface with abrasive paper.

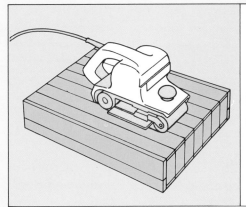

9
Sand the surfaces smooth.

10

Saw the lid of the case loose, using the circular saw and rip fence. Remember that there must be room for the hinges and locks in the top of the case.

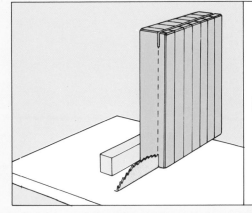

10
Saw the lid loose.

11

In order to make the lid fit into the case exactly, guide rails (a) must be fitted. These are made from lathes, about 6 mm (¼″) thick. Drill tiny holes in the rails so that they don't split when you nail and glue them in place.

(b) The guide rails must protrude about 3 mm (⅛″) above the edge of the case.

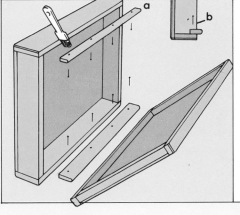

11
Add guide rails.

12

Mark up the male and female parts of each hinge from one piece of wood and saw them out, using the rip fence and a push stick to guide the workpiece. Saw along the dotted lines.

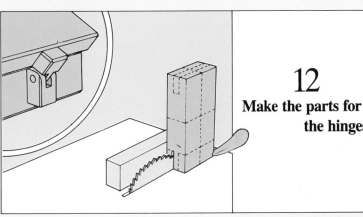

12
Make the parts for the hinges.

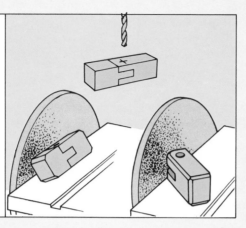

13

Drill holes for the hinges' central pins.

13

Assemble the male and female parts of each hinge and drill a hole in each for the central pin. This should be where the male's tenon diagonals intersect (marked with a cross on the upper illustration). Round the back of each hinge and bevel the sides on a grinding disc.

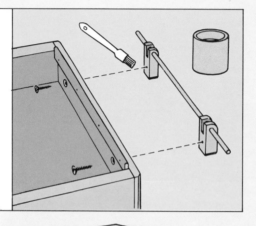

14

Fit on the female part of each hinge.

14

A metal rod with the same diameter as the central pin helps you to align the hinges in relation to each other. Glue and screw the female parts to the case, so that their tops are flush with the top of the case.

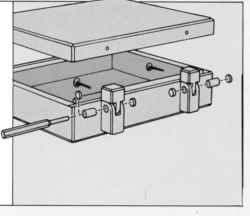

15

Assemble the complete hinges.

15

Cut two pieces from the metal rod, using the hacksaw. Each piece should be about 6 mm (¼″) shorter than the width of the hinge. Assemble the male and female parts of the hinges and insert the pieces of the rod. Conceal the metal ends with wooden plugs.

16

Mark up the case handle on a piece of wood. Wooden plugs driven through angled holes in the handle and case top will fasten the handle to the case. Mark up these holes. Then start the holes with a stoppered drill. Now cramp the workpiece at the correct angle in an upright pillar drill and bore the final holes.

Cramp the handle in place on the lid. Drill through the angled holes so that the holes in the case have the same angle as those in the handle.

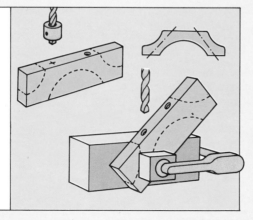

16

Mark up and drill holes in the workpiece for the case's handle.
Drill holes in the case top.

17

Cut out the handle with the bandsaw. Smooth the handle to its final shape with abrasive paper. Spread adhesive on suitable plugs and in the bored holes. Using a mallet, tap the plugs through the bored holes in the handle and the case, thus fixing the handle to the case.

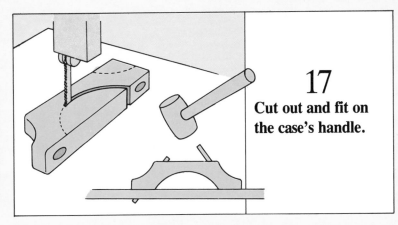

17
Cut out and fit on the case's handle.

18

Mark up and bore holes in the lid for the lock plugs. Glue and tap the plugs into place with the mallet.

18
Fit on the lock plugs.

19

Make a template (*a*) for the lock. Put the template over the plug in the lid and mark up the axis. Bore a hole for the axle of each lock, which will be a wood screw of suitable dimension. The bored holes must be of slightly greater dimension than that of the screws, as the screw must be able to turn freely with the lock.

Use a chisel to cut out a suitable hole so that the lock will fit smoothly over the lock plug.

19
Make the locks.

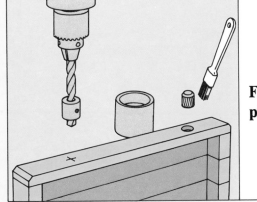

20

Screw the locks in place. Insert a Teflon washer between the screw head and the case to facilitate opening and closing the lock.

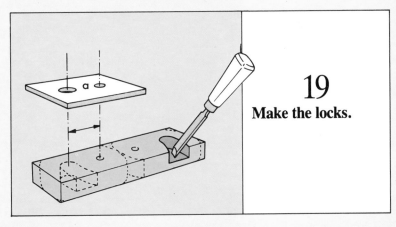

Finishing

A softwood like pine should be given a protective coating of a two-component lacquer. If the surface becomes pitted and dented, you can always sand it down to a new smooth finish and give it a new coat of lacquer.

With a hardwood, all you have to do is to oil the surface with, say, teak oil.

20
Screw the locks into place.

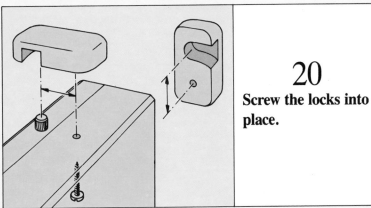

149

TURNING

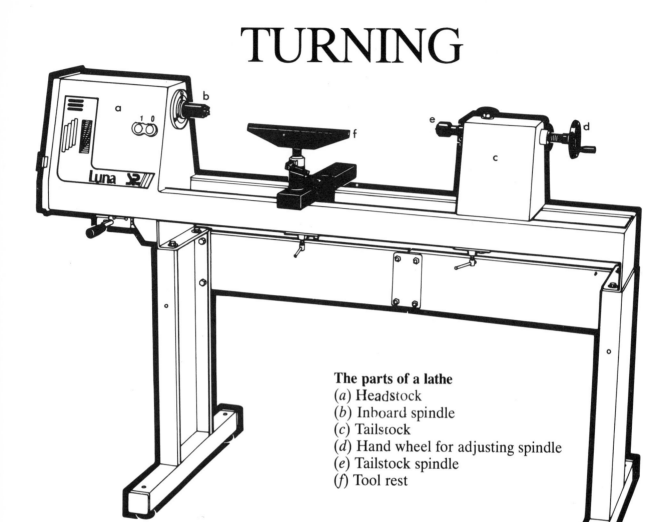

The parts of a lathe
(*a*) Headstock
(*b*) Inboard spindle
(*c*) Tailstock
(*d*) Hand wheel for adjusting spindle
(*e*) Tailstock spindle
(*f*) Tool rest

The Turning Lathe

The lathe is the only woodworking machine in which the workpiece rather than the tool is driven. It is also one of the most dangerous machines and must be treated with great respect. Always follow the basic safety rules.

1. Never mount a square or rectangular turning blank (the workpiece) wider than 50 mm (2″) in the lathe. It must first be sawn or planed into an octagon.
2. Your tool rest should be as near the blank as possible and centred horizontally on it. If you are face-plate turning, you need to have the tool rest a little above centre.

3. Your cutting tools must always be sharp. Remember that the tools that have a flat edge are easiest to handle. Gouges with rounded edges are more difficult to handle and demand more skill, but in return they produce a smoother surface. Never use gouges when you are turning the inside of a blank.
4. The wood in the turning blank must be free of defects.
5. Use your commonsense and keep your fingers away from the moving parts. Don't have loose clothing, jewelry, or hair that could get caught in the lathe. And roll up your sleeves!

Smoothing

When you have finished turning the blank, you will want to smooth the piece to a fine finish. Always remove the tool rest, so that you don't get your fingers caught between it and the blank. Fold the abrasive paper in two or three, or use a grinding block, so that you don't get your fingers burnt.

Start with rough abrasive paper and then change to a finer grade. As a final check, dampen the wood with a wet cloth and smooth down again, when the fibres have risen.

Choosing wood for turning

The wood should be free from defects and as seasoned as possible. Check the yearly rings. Trees grow differently in the spring and autumn, and the growth rings can differ a lot. Use a piece on which the autumn rings are as equal as possible to the spring rings.

The best woods are birch, ash, beech, yew, teak, sycamore, maple, and American black walnut. Pine is soft and easy to work with, and has fine patterns. Oak gives a beautiful finish but is tough on tool edges.

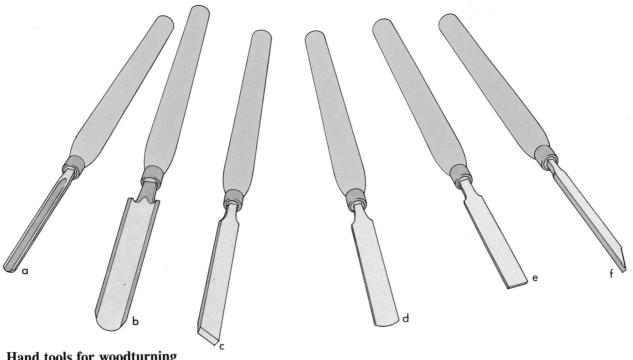

Hand tools for woodturning

The following is the basic kit of hand tools and measuring tools that you need for turning in wood. As usual, buy good-quality tools and they will last a long time and do a good job for you.

(*a*) Spindle gouge
(*b*) Roughing gouge
(*c*) Skew chisel
(*d*) Round-nosed scraper
(*e*) Square-nosed scraper
(*f*) Parting tool
(*g*) Outside calipers
(*h*) Inside calipers

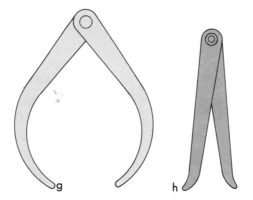

FRUIT BOWL

MATERIAL
any of the woods mentioned on the
previous page

TOOLS
lathe
gouges and chisels
depth gauge
marking gauge
inside and outside calipers
wing compass
wing dividers
wood mallet

1

Choose a suitable piece of wood. Plane one face and one edge.

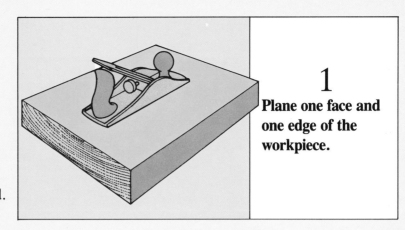

1

Plane one face and one edge of the workpiece.

2

Saw the workpiece in two with the circular saw. Continue to saw it up into smaller pieces until all the pieces have a width of about 70 mm (3″).

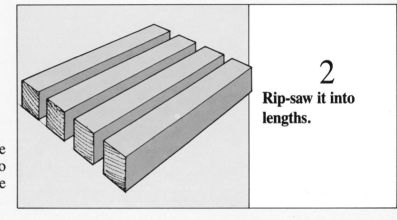

2

Rip-saw it into lengths.

3

Plane all the pieces and glue them together with phenolic resin glue. When the glue has cured, plane one face and one edge.

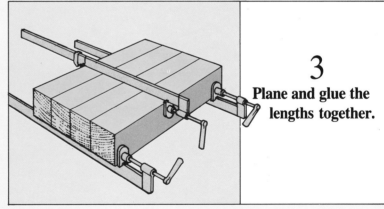

3

Plane and glue the lengths together.

4

Use a wing compass to mark up the outer contour of the bowl. With the same centre, draw another circle with the same radius as that of the face plate. This second circle will help you to position the turning blank when you are screwing it onto the face plate.

Use the bandsaw to saw along the outer diameter of the bowl. You have now a turning blank that will be relatively well balanced.

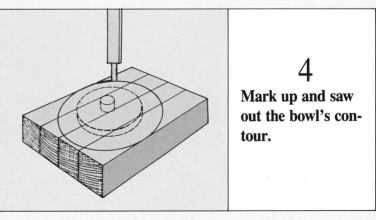

4

Mark up and saw out the bowl's contour.

5

Screw the turning blank to the face plate.

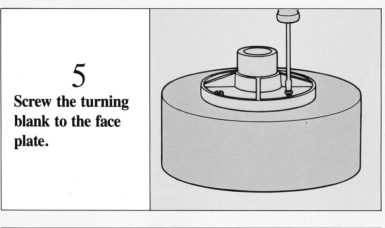

5

Mount the blank on the face plate with at least four screws.

6

Rough-turn the outside.

7

Shape the outside and make the plinth.

8

Measure the plinth exactly.

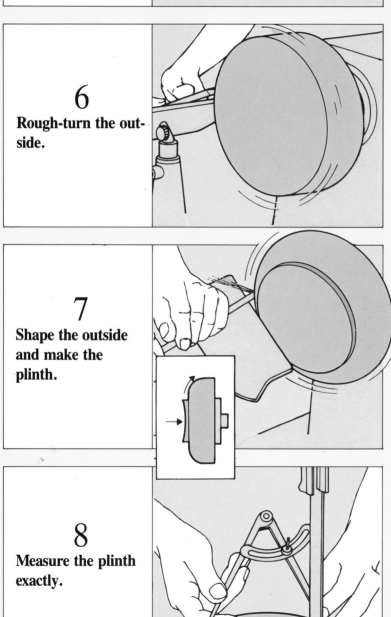

6

Start the lathe and, with the tool rest a little above centre, rough-turn the blank into balance, using a 10 mm (⅜″) roughing gouge.

7

Continue turning and shaping the outer contour of the bowl.

Because the inside of the bowl is quite deep, you need to have a plinth on the bottom of the bowl which will fit into a female base, or scrap plate, to hold the bowl tightly while you are turning the inside. This plinth will also serve as the bowl's stand.

Shape a cylindrical plinth (at least 10 mm, or ⅜″, high) on the base of the bowl, using a gouge when you are cutting in the round and a chisel when you are cutting straight.

The bottom of the plinth should be somewhat concave, as in the small drawing.

8

Measure the diameter and height of the plinth, using a wing dividers and a depth gauge.

9

From a sturdy piece of waste wood, make a female base for the plinth of the bowl. This must fit very tightly around the plinth, holding it firmly while the inside of the bowl is being turned.

Screw the piece of waste wood (*a*), which is to be the base, to the face plate and rough-turn it until it is in balance.

Mark up the diameter of the plinth on the base.

Turn the base with a chisel, so that the recess you make equals the shape of the plinth exactly.

10

The depth and diameter of the turned recess must be exact, and the plinth on the bottom of the bowl must fit tightly into it.

If you must adjust the measurements, use a chisel, working very lightly. Check the fit of the plinth regularly—you should end up with a "suction grip".

11

Before you join the plinth and the base, dampen the base's edges. The wood fibres will then swell a little and grip the plinth when it is inserted.

12

Press the plinth into position immediately. Tap it in with the mallet. You are now ready to turn the inside of the bowl.

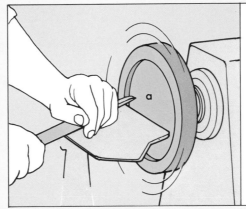

9

Turn a recess in a piece of waste to form a base.

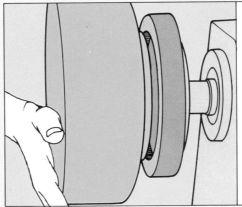

10

Check that the plinth fits into the base.

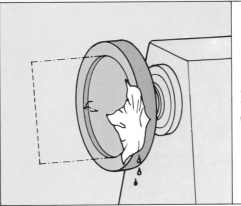

11

Dampen the edges of the base.

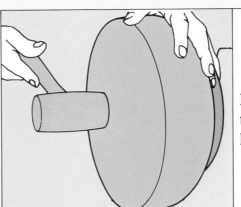

12

Fit the plinth into the base and tap home.

13

Finish the outside of the bowl.

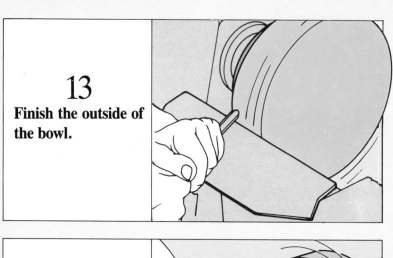

13

First, finish turning the outside of the bowl, using a gouge.

14

Mark out the thickness of the bown with a parting tool.

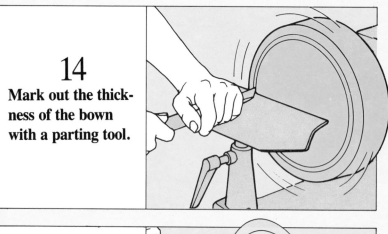

14

Adjust the tool rest for inside turning. Use a parting tool to cut down the inside to the correct thickness. Work only with the point of the tool.

15

Start the inside turning by making a shallow hole.

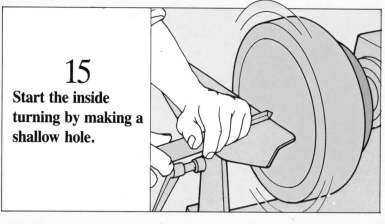

15

Press the parting tool in towards the centre and make a shallow hole.

16

Turn the inside of the bowl.

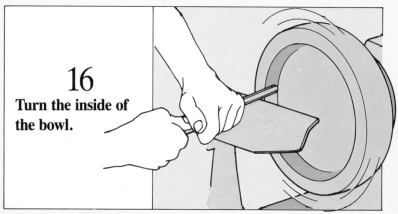

16

You can now begin to work out the insides of the bowl. Follow the wood's fibre direction and work preferably with a narrow chisel. Work slowly and methodically, holding the chisel in a steady grip. Make the shallow central hole deeper, and check the depth.

17

Check the inner measurements. Always stop the lathe when measuring. The outside minus the inside heights give the thickness of the bottom of the bowl.

17

Check the inside measurements. Stop the lathe!

18

Change to the tool rest for inside turning, to improve access to the inside of the bowl during the final turning.

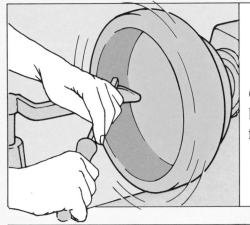

18

Change to an inboard tool rest and finish the inside.

19

Remove the tool rest and smooth the bowl with abrasive paper folded in three. When polishing the inside of the bowl, support your polishing hand as shown.

Remove the bowl from the base and smooth the bottom of the plinth.

19

Smooth the bowl with abrasive paper.

Finishing

Treat the polished bowl with paraffin oil or a coat of varnish. The former is best if the bowl is to be used as a salad bowl, while varnish will protect the wood against stains from certain types of citrus fruits.

DISH

MATERIAL
a hard type of wood, such as ash, for
  the scrap plate
pine or similar for the dish

TOOLS
lathe
gouges and chisels

You can turn a blank inboards as well as outboards by using the following method.

1

Make a scrap plate and mount it on the face plate.

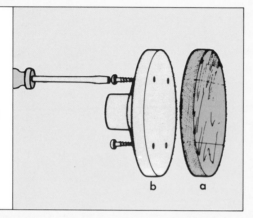

1

Make a scrap plate (*a*) from hard wood and screw it onto the face plate (*b*) with at least four screws. Rough-turn the scrap plate so that it is brought to a true circle.

2

Glue paper onto the scrap plate and spread glue on the paper.

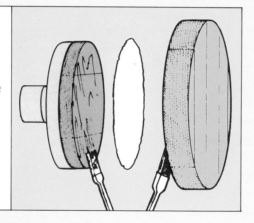

2

Cover the scrap plate with glue. Cut out a suitable piece of paper and place it on the glued surface. Cover the upper surface of the paper with glue.

Now spread glue on the turning blank, which you sawed out earlier on the circular saw or bandsaw.

3

Glue the turning blank to the paper and mount onto the headstock.

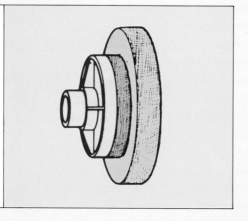

3

Press the blank against the glued paper. Allow the glue to dry properly.

Note! It is important that the blank is centred on the scrap plate, so mark up the bottom diameter of the scrap plate on the blank, so that you have a line to follow when positioning it.

Attach the face plate with the glued-on blank to the headstock. Rough-turn the outside of the blank to get the piece in balance.

4

Turn the outer shape of the dish with a gouge.

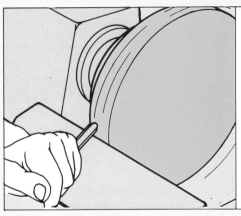

4

Form the outer shape of the dish.

5

Now turn the inside of the dish with a chisel. Use a round-nosed scraper to finish off. Be careful with the thin walls.

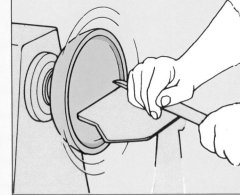

5

Turn the inside.

6

Remove the tool rest. Smooth and finish with abrasive paper. Then polish it with wood polish or paraffin.

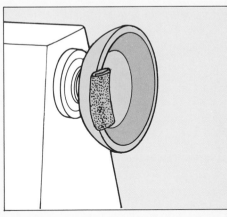

6

Smooth and finish the surface.

7

Remove the dish from the scrap plate by pressing a chisel gently between them at the glue line.

Clean off any dried glue by smoothing with abrasive paper. Smooth the bottom of the dish.

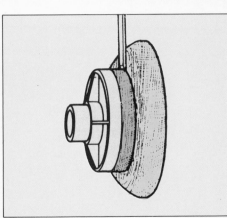

7

Separate the dish from the scrap plate.

THE WOODWORKER'S MANUAL
has been typeset in Times on the Linotype system
in 11/12 points Normal, 12/14 points Bold,
and 24 points Normal.
The book has been printed by offset printing
on 115 gsm woodfree Litolux offset paper.
The cover is covered in Imitlin Paglierino.